DISCOVERING POSSIBILITY

A Common Sense Conservative Manifesto
(For Classical Liberals Too)

KEVIN J. KERVICK

ISBN: 1456327267
ISBN-13: 9781456327262

For Lauren and Brian

My favorite Millennials and two of America's future leaders

CONTENTS

The Unfolding Process
Making America Cool Again
Destroying the Hippie Fantasy
Realistic Optimism on the Rise
The People Rule

FOREWORD

An accidental combination of experience and interest will often reveal events to one man under aspects, which few yet see. – F. A. Hayek.

It is with satisfaction that I have the opportunity to introduce Kevin Kervick and this book, *Discovering Possibility: A Common Sense Conservative Manifesto (For Classical Liberals Too)*. I am not a public figure, nor do I possess the formal credentials that would convey the normal status one typically holds to write about such a heady topic as humanistic classical liberalism. However, a chance meeting with Kevin has provided me with the opportunity to contribute to a project that is important to me. While I do not hold academic credentials as an economist, historian, political scientist, psychologist, or sociologist, I do offer the categorical expertise of being human and an appreciation of what is involved to be free and truly responsible for my own affairs.

I connected with Kevin and his organization, A Place for Possibilities, through social networking. I can say I am relieved. The philosophy behind A Place for Possibilities that Kevin articulates in this book contains a set of interrelated concepts the liberty community tends to overlook. Indeed, with the recent success in the 2010 mid-term congressional elections, the reasonable arguments presented in this book are gaining in importance as conservative intellectuals and political leaders grapple with what to do next, during what some observers are already calling the post-Obama or post-progressive era.

Based on my recent first-hand experience as a field worker inside Kentucky Senator Rand Paul's successful political campaign, I believe there is a growing impetus in the United States to spread the fundamental American principles of personal responsibility and limited government. I believe this new momentum will create a monumental cultural shift that will alter the way many Americans view their government and the nature of their communities. I was not able to outline exactly how that process might unfold on a national scale until I was able to see this plan laid out by Kevin. At its core, the issue is the mistaken belief that traditional conservative arguments are the only ideas that will further liberty. Kevin has put forward a common sense philosophy that upholds many of those traditional ideals but also includes a modern humanistic emphasis that more accurately honors the wisdom of the Founding Fathers. My belief is that we community builders must help our fellow citizens embrace a personal philosophy of liberty, not just as it relates to a framework of government but as it relates to a framework of understanding human frustration, starting with their own. Both Kevin and I want to help people embrace a common sense conservative ethos in their own lives and at the same time, help them manage the existential anxiety that comes from thinking and living freely and being responsible for one's actions.

Despite having what I believe are the correct ideas, I am certain the liberty community, especially as represented by the Tea Party Movement, is woefully prepared, on a person-by-person basis, to own their own anxieties and handle them in constructive ways. I hope liberty activists will find *Discovering Possibility* helpful in building the traits of charity and community in addition to the predominantly freedom-centered values of contemporary libertarians. Furthermore, since big government enables both Conservatives and Progressives, it will not be enough to only advance the seminal arguments of scholars such as Hayek, Lewis, or Rand because those works have already found like-minded audiences. The liberty community will need to look to fresh perspectives in order to broaden its appeal.

My first hand experience has shown me that we will need a modern iteration of those classic ideas to reach contemporary audiences who tend to think with a corrupted mindset that has been so completely contaminated by big government propaganda. It will not be easy to change hearts and minds, especially since the increasing polarization in the country has stifled open-mindedness and diminished the human impulse to live freely and to be charitable. The desire for each, even amongst the liberty community to control and plan away their own anxieties and thus control and plan others is the societal norm.

However, with Kevin's outline in *Discovering Possibility* as a guide, if a few people begin to engage in this effort and they establish relationships of trust with those around them, there will be a growing support network to help others act courageously and with purpose. A support network will be necessary because most people are inherently resistant to change. Logic and reason without support will fail in opening people to the possibilities for change and helping them actualize their intentions. The establishment of free, voluntary, and supportive relationships is the only real avenue to enduring cultural change. Change in one form or another, is coming to our communities and that change will have far-reaching effects.

My age situates me at the extreme leading edge of a generation of individuals born in the United States between 1980 and 2000. Kevin dedicated an entire chapter to the possibilities of my generation. Termed Millennials by generational theorists, and forecasted by many to be the next great American generation, my peers have some distinguishing characteristics that Kevin describes in depth in Chapter Six. I would like to highlight one notable millennial trait, which is that we Millennials are not predisposed to rigid or close-minded thinking. More importantly, we are open to new ideas but only if the ideas appeal to our sensibilities, and maintain a sense of practicality and reasonableness. While we tend to be freedom loving, the central controlling nature of big government and its cultural extensions have depressed our natural human tendencies to seek freedom and to act responsibly. Thus, although we embrace new ideas and new directions, or even rediscovered ones, including classical liberalism, adopting a liberty mindset and lifestyle will be challenging for us.

Many Millennials were swept up by the mythical hope and change of the 2008 Obama presidential campaign and later many of them became leaders in the Progressive Movement.

However, a quieter segment of that same group had a different perspective. That group of young adults found themselves as intellectual leaders of the Tea Party Movement in early 2009, seemingly out of place amongst the older participants. I was one of those leaders.

I had seen the core ideals that were later embraced by the Tea Party Movement take root in Ron Paul's electric 2008 presidential run. I had seen that simmering frustration express itself in the early 2009 Tea Party events. Later, I witnessed how a principled philosophy based on liberty can act as a political faith to under gird a successful campaign in Rand Paul's successful US Senate race. However, most concerning for me was that despite adhering to that philosophy, and despite being wildly successful on the front lines in advancing the conservative agenda in the 2010 midterm elections, the liberty movement remained on shaky footing. Despite the momentum and success, many of the supporters of liberty quickly dismissed many of the concepts I support and that Kevin also discusses in this Common Sense Conservative Manifesto, at the first hint of disappointment.

I saw from inside Rand Paul's campaign headquarters before and after the GOP primary that the ability of individual supporters to cope with the frustrations that come from revolutionary change is limited. In the face of running a winnable campaign, a candidate cannot acknowledge all of the concerns expressed by his supporters. In the case of many of Paul's supporters, there was a rock solid faith in a philosophy and belief in a well-adjusted candidate. However, even this principled group had no shortage of toxic episodes during which they had difficulty trusting campaign staff and other supporters to uphold the principles to which they aspired. They were looking to a candidate, Paul, to reinforce those ideas, but for political reasons he was unable to articulate all of them. Furthermore, the effects of a barrage of media appearances that became controversial had strained his ability to soothe the discontent of his supporters. Hence, the supporters had to support themselves.

There have been hundreds of articles written about the origins of the Tea Party Movement. In my opinion, many mainstream Americans see the Tea Party Movement and its membership as aberrations. Participants themselves are frustrated, often portrayed by the more superficial media reports as single slogan, sound-bite machines, decrying the scope and size of the federal government as "unconstitutional". Some of the more mindful representatives will be able to elaborate that the Tea Partiers are seeking a return to the rule of law. Some, who are more disposed to classical liberalism, like Kevin, emphasize both the missing spirit and the intent of the constitutional framework. The astute might be able to articulate a root cause of the Tea Party Movement frustration, which is that any time government overreaches into a "gray area" that is not specifically enumerated in the constitution it is just as likely to be construed as arbitrary rather than as fair and just.

An individual's perception of fairness and justice will ebb and flow and is highly subjective from person to person. Each person's emotional upbringing and life experiences define his/her ability to cope with frustration, and that accumulated emotional history directly influences his/her perception of fairness. With better information and corresponding psychological containment that Kevin hopes to offer in this book (and I am addressing in my own upcoming thesis), free people will have a more charitable definition of what constitutes fairness and a better ability to cope with frustration. Under a lack of psychological containment or the reverse, psychological tyranny, fairness becomes a never-ending and confusing mandate in a world of arbitrary restrictions.

I believe Kevin is ahead of his time with the release of *Discovering Possibility*. He understands that the greatest challenge to civilization, if free people with differing viewpoints are to coexist peacefully, is the lack of a set of unifying principles. This book offers such a set of principles that are firmly grounded in enlightenment thinking while smartly ignoring talk of political victory or dictating tribal partisan policy positions. Politics often attracts the most outspoken personalities seeking to advance narrow agendas. Unfortunately, in this era of hyper-competitive partisanship and entrenched government power, politics has all to often become an end unto itself. This book is an attempt to put the horse before the cart.

This book also highlights why we are a people that are not meeting our obligations to act in a personally responsible way and to be good neighbors. Kevin and I believe there can be no lasting political change without the underlying social change to support it. Knowing the composition of those in the Tea Party Movement about as well as anyone, I can state, based on first-hand knowledge that I do not believe the Tea Party Movement has a comprehensive social change philosophy that ties it together. Much of the membership does not even possess a comprehensive understanding of the philosophy of classical liberalism that is at the root of the American system. Thus, to create enduring social change, members of the Tea Party Movement will need to adopt an accessible personal philosophy or creed and make that philosophy real in their own lives. In *Discovering Possibility*, Kevin offers such a working philosophy.

This book touts common sense, and indeed in the realm of normal relationships built on trust and mutual responsibility, common sense reigns. In early colonial America, where people had no choice but to be independent, and active in mutually supporting communities, common sense was abundant. Kevin is thus advocating something enduring and simple, but at the same time, revolutionary, just as these ideas were in the late eighteenth century.

I witnessed many fascinating interpersonal dynamics during the robust 2010 campaign for Rand Paul. I was fortunate that those dynamics paralleled a period of dramatic change in my own life, and I was thus able to apply what I was learning about personality and human organization to my own personal journey. Frankly, the campaign opportunity allowed me to participate as a leader among a group of passionate people who were often frustrated and uncertain about the future.

All of us who volunteered on the campaign knew we were involved in something big. Even though we were uncertain about precisely what would unfold in the future, we intrinsically knew that furthering this exciting collection of ideas and electing this exemplary candidate and many more like him, would be how liberty would ultimately thrive in

America again. I am grateful that Kevin has been able to honor the cause of liberty we were fighting for in the Rand Paul campaign by articulating the challenge we faced then, and continue to face today as we endeavor to advance the cause of liberty. As importantly, I am grateful that Kevin has proposed a change process in a way that I could not do myself, which has opened the door for my own thinking about how I would like to continue to be involved in the next phase of my journey.

Change is likely the only certainty in a truly free and voluntary society. Destructive change is the hallmark of a tyrannical one. Every individual has two choices – to be as open and receptive to that change as possible, or to resist change and prolong the difficulty. Openness to change for you may start with adopting the common sense solutions outlined in this book or you may discover a different avenue. Nevertheless, change is unavoidable.

While the thesis in this book might seem incorrect, inconsequential, or even despicable to some of you at first glance, I would urge you to give the ideas a chance before you reject them outright. You may feel disloyal to other ideas or people, or anxious about the implications, but over-time the ideas may make sense to you. They did for me. I am encouraged that if taken seriously, Kevin Kervick's ideas have the potential to shine the way for people to be individual examples of liberty that the rest of the world will want to emulate.

Mike Wallace - January 2011

PREFACE

I started writing this book several years ago at a time when I was quite frustrated with the status quo in my profession. From my perspective, the human services landscape had become a bureaucratized behemoth. Social services were increasingly embedded within what had become a jobs program for an ever-growing legion of well-intentioned helpers that were part of the services sector economy, the fastest growing segment of the U.S. economy.

The problem I confronted was the ineffectiveness of many of the services that were designed for folks most in need. In my opinion, we had created an inefficient and self-perpetuating bureaucratic juggernaut that was burning out its increasingly disillusioned workers at very high rates. I had become one of the disillusioned and decided that in order to keep my sanity I needed to figure out a different way to contribute. That was the beginning of this phase of my life and the impetus for the founding of *Responsive Community Resources*, a community-building organization, that would eventually become the current-day educational nonprofit corporation, *A Place for Possibilities*.

At the same time, I was in a state of professional brownout from the all too common family therapist occupational hazard that eventually leaves many of us unsatisfied with helping one individual, or one family at a time. I was vividly seeing the connection between individual and family pathology and larger community patterns, which lead me to working as a community family therapist who frequently tried to help families see how their own troubles were connected to what was going on around them. From that level of abstraction I ventured into the world of capacity building in which I operated as a de facto community family therapist, attempting to stimulate culture changes that I believed would contribute to a healthier and happier community in which people would require fewer professional services.

By now the reader has undoubtedly predicted the next phase of remedy for my occupational hazard affliction, which was to look even larger, to the (declining) American culture itself as a source of discontent and disillusionment for many. Since then I have decided to take my community building to a higher level of abstraction and attempt to be a catalyst for culture change at the level of the American community at large. That decision in 2005 stimulated a reformulation of the mission and goals of A Place for Possibilities, and it is the basis of this book, which I had originally subtitled, *Restoring the American Community by Rediscovering Freedom, Personal Responsibility, Neighborliness, and Thrift.* That is where I am today, attempting to be a voice for restoration of the core American values that I believe lead to personal happiness and community wellbeing.

Thus, the purpose of *Discovering Possibility* is to provide inspiration to current and future generations of Americans. My intent is to describe my view of our Founders' intentions, illustrate where we have been, where we are today, and outline a new path for America that will restore the country to its founding ideals, the wisdom of which will, in turn lead to the aforementioned personal happiness and community wellbeing.

I would like the reader to know this has been a personal transformation for me. I have evolved from a wide-eyed professional helper who was very much connected to the progressive political orthodoxy that under-girds much of the professional culture in human services, to a right-leaning American Communitarian who believes the Progressive Movement in America is one of the root causes of community devolution and personal unhappiness. For a lot of reasons, not the least of which is being a father and husband trying to raise a decent family in the midst of what has seemed like a declining culture all around me, I have come to abandon the Progressive ideology that dominated my earlier thinking. I see myself as a Common Sense Conservative influenced by the Deism and Classical Liberalism of the American Founders, which is a worldview I will advance throughout the book. In my view, Common Sense Conservatism is the new centrist position in the United States because the associated socio-political worldview characterizes the thinking of the majority of Americans. My hope is this book might offer a balanced and realistic vision for people that might be on the socio-political fence looking for a refreshing common sense alternative to the polarized tribal condition that defines so much of the national discourse today. These are consequential times that require enlightened solutions that honor the legacy of our founding.

I would like to add another note about my process. Like the Millennials I am trying to inspire, I fully embrace the freedom and power of the Internet as a revolutionary communication and research tool. Internet media are the modern day printing press. Thus, in the writing of this book I tried to capture the full power of that medium to do my research. Additionally, our organization is committed to tapping into the vast opportunities presented by the myriad of on-line communication vehicles for education and social marketing.

INTRODUCTION

Restoring America - A Place for Possibilities

I believe one's socio-political philosophy and spirituality contribute to the values and habits that lead to his personal happiness. Additionally, the application of those habits on a wider scale forms the basis of the health of the community. Therefore, in *Discovering Possibility*, I am attempting to offer a complete socio-political-spiritual synthesis for the reader in the form of a rediscovered and bold Common Sense Conservative Manifesto.

The basis of the Manifesto is that the Founders of the United States of America believed there were self-evident Truths that come from Nature's God. Although the United States is not a Christian nation it is a nation that was founded on the belief that citizen rights come from something larger than man. The United States is also a nation that requires its citizens to exercise their God-given freedom in a responsible way and to be good neighbors. In this book, I offer a roadmap for the rediscovery and reactivation of these essential notions in order to limit central government and restore the civil society. As the civil society is reinvigorated, more Americans will find happiness and more communities will thrive. This is the essence of the Common Sense Conservative Movement in America, which is fundamentally, a back to basics restoration of the timeless values and habits that will make America thrive in the twenty-first century.

During this age of government expansion and declining personal responsibility I am increasingly attracted to the Libertarian thesis, which is reflected above, but unlike some Libertarians I strongly emphasize the necessity of voluntary social responsibility, which I refer to as neighborliness in this book. In my opinion, political Progressives and social justice advocates have illegitimately changed the meaning of neighborliness. They believe government has a moral responsibility to take from some people in order to give to others in order to right the wrongs of the past. Neighborliness, from my perspective, is by definition voluntary, which is a point of view I will delve into more deeply later in the book.

As importantly, unlike some Philosophical Communitarians and Progressives, I do not support the twentieth century concept of positive rights[1] because I believe our rights come solely from Nature's God (which mirrors the Deistic emphasis and Classical Liberalism of many of the prominent Founding Fathers), and not from government, individuals, or even the community itself. In my opinion, one person or one community does not have the moral authority to demand a right from another and no surrogate authority can demand positive rights on another's behalf. I believe individuals within communities have the moral authority to decide how they will exercise their freedom in order to build healthy communities AND find personal happiness, which reflects a uniquely American style of Communitarianism. More simply stated, I am advocating that the American community needs to restore a heavy dose of liberty with an equally strong emphasis on voluntary neighborliness, which was the original American foundation.

I believe there is a fundamental American identity that was established at the time of our founding, is buttressed by our Constitution, and has been sustained by our cultural heritage for over two hundred and thirty years. America has been gradually losing her identity. My belief is that our mission as patriotic community builders, citizen leaders, and culture change agents is the deconstruction of the social, cultural, and institutional forces that do not stem from or fortify the essential American values that make up our identity, so we can rebuild our communities in a way that reinforces that fundamental American ideal.

Our mission pre-dated the consciousness-raising of the Tea Party Movement in America, which I see as a Conservative Populist social movement that has bubbled up in response to the progressive ideology, out of control spending, corporate bailouts, and crony capitalism that Tea Partiers believe are threatening the American identity.

The majority of the original Tea Party protesters in 2009 were Libertarians, many of them younger Ron Paul supporters, who formed the intellectual basis of the movement, which had a strong limited government creed.[2] Later, as the movement became more popular and as healthcare took center stage as a key rallying cry issue, the movement attracted older, more traditional contemporary Conservatives, many of who also came with their socially conservative values.

Fundamentally, the Tea Party Movement is a limited government protest that exists because many people believe the United States of America is on the wrong track and has strayed from its Constitutional roots.[3]

As part of the research for this book I went to one of the first Tea Party rallies in America at Boston Commons on April 15, 2009, and knew immediately this was going to grow into one of the most significant social movements of my lifetime. It was a spirited, patriotic event that concluded later in the day at the Boston Harbor with a reenactment of the original 1773 Tea Party protest. I was stirred by the unabashed patriotism and revolutionary goals of the presenters. I have been to five other events since that great day at one of the seats of American freedom and I have followed the movement closely.

This book is more encompassing than other works that offer a narrowly focused Tea Party Manifesto but I do appreciate the restorative spirit that is at the heart of that movement. *Discovering Possibility* intends to go beyond mere political and economic reform and into the spiritual, philosophical, and psychological restoration that will be necessary if America is to get back on track. Thus, by using the term, Common Sense Conservatism, I am trying to connect the reader to the Classical Liberalism of the Founders, which makes this book both conservative and liberal in a classical sense. It includes the enduring values that are most often associated with traditional conservatism today and the openness to experience and creative energy that is usually associated with liberalism, and characterized the attitude of many of America's Founders, who were products of the age of reason.

While the terms are often used interchangeably, the age of reason, which preceded the Age of Enlightenment, is seen as an era whose thinkers, many of them English rather than French, were more accepting of tradition as a source of community wisdom than the Age of Enlightenment. Enlightenment thinkers tended to be more hostile to tradition and produced the more violent, anti-establishment, French Revolution. I believe the American Revolution and the ideas that stimulated the founding of the United States are more accurately placed within the historical parameters of the age of reason rather than the Age of Enlightenment, which came later and was more radical. However, I believe it is also accurate to say the American Founders were operating from a set of *enlightened principles* that were also closely associated with and stimulated other thinkers and revolutionaries who later would be considered products of the Age of Enlightenment in a broad sense. I offer the above point of clarification in order to be as historically accurate as possible, although throughout the book there may be instances where these terms overlap.

In Part One of the book, I define my interpretation of what I believe the Founding Fathers intended when they created the United States of America. The American community that grew from that heritage has a distinct identity based on the fundamental American values that created the norms of the civil society.

The American version of the civil society is inextricably linked to the Deistic emphasis (Nature's God) the Founders used to justify our liberties from government and as an alternative to state-controlled religion, both institutions of which had consumed man's liberty throughout history. The Founders understood well that an aspiring Republic would need some unifying elements even if there were disparate religious groups throughout the Colonies. Thus, I advocate for a rediscovery of Deism as a connective tissue among the different religious expressions in America.

In addition, in Part One, I draw from my own life history as a citizen in small town America and from my extensive domestic and international travel to illustrate my beliefs about the American community. After defining the fundamentals of the American community, I describe how I believe the civil society in America is deteriorating as many Americans have discarded the core values that I talk about in more detail later in the book.

Part One concludes with a challenge to members of the Millennial Generation to accept a great mission, which, from my perspective, is to help our citizens rediscover our identity and restore our communities so the United States can remain an exceptional nation and world leader. The Millennials tend to be realistic optimists as the recent *Rally to Restore Sanity (and Fear)* in Washington D.C. illustrated and has been documented elsewhere.[4] Being reasonable in the face of fear mongering and extremism was the over-riding theme of that day and a trait that will serve Millennials well as they accept the reigns of an American culture that many believe is dysfunctional.

Since my professional background is in family therapy and community building, I can write with some authority based on that experience about how I believe freedom, personal responsibility, neighborliness, and thrift, the core

American values I chose to emphasize in Part Two of the book, lead to individual happiness and community health. When one practices in the trenches for over twenty years as I have, many patterns consistently emerge, which provides an ethnographic frame of inquiry. It is primarily from that experience and the experiences I have had traveling around the world during the past five years that I draw many of the conclusions in this section of the book.

Part Three of the book outlines a deconstruction and renewal plan I believe will contribute to a better America. I am adding my voice to the chorus of modern day deconstructors and rebuilders who believe we are in a critical period in our Nation's development and the time is now to reclaim our essential identity in order to restore America.

Many politicians are shouting to their constituent groups that we must cut spending but few are actually suggesting concrete ways to do it. In this section, I suggest concrete steps we can take to curtail government spending and to revive the economy. I describe how these cuts will lead to temporary pain for some citizens but resultant changes will deconstruct an out of control government and restore a sense of personal responsibility and thrift.

Throughout *Discovering Possibility* the reader will see the phrase, *common sense wisdom,* to describe my ideas because in addition to seeing myself as someone that seeks wisdom and Truth, I like the inferred connection to the work of Thomas Paine that the phrase, *common sense* connotes. My hope is readers will accept the ideas in the humble way I strive to present them, with my belief that there are no new ideas, only recirculations and repackaging of the wisdom of the ages. As a discoverer and a synthesizer trying to make a living, my job is to find good ideas and create connections between them that make sense in the search for a happy and productive life. I claim no superior intelligence or better access to wisdom. I am merely spending more time on the discovery, synthesis and delivery system.

Finally, my belief is that most people are attracted to ideas that are accessible to them for snapshot moments in time and they strive to incorporate them when the ideas fit with their own internal synthesis. So, these humble offerings come in the spirit of sowing the seeds and sharing the wealth of rediscovered community wisdom and hoping that any of the ideas fit for a particular reader.

PART ONE

The American Community

Some people argue there is no such thing as an American community. They believe the United States is simply a collection of many disparate communities with different cultural identities and allegiances. This is the doctrine of multiculturalism, which holds that several different cultures (rather than one national culture) can coexist peacefully and equitably in a single country. In essence, according to this view, there is no distinctly American culture or identity. I believe that view is misguided. I not only believe in the existence of the American community but also in the concept of American exceptionalism.

I believe there is something unique and special about America that came together at the time of our founding, when enlightened and courageous men and women discovered and codified the accumulated wisdom of the ages to advance Western Civilization. There was a nexus of ideas, motivation, and righteous energy that some believe was Divine Providence. Others believe it was powerful synergy, that spurned the birth of a grand new experiment, which endures two hundred thirty-five years later. The Founders were not simply a collection of pragmatic lawyers and politicians as some revisionists suggest. Most of them were courageous idealists who became the carriers of the best ideas of the time and were inspired to make a lasting impact on humanity, and they did.

Belief in American exceptionalism does not preclude the idea that other nations are not also exceptional. Exceptionalism merely gives Americans something in which to feel pride. Pride is not the same as arrogance. Pride allows one to honor and support his/her cultural identity so the most important aspects of that identity are likely to be perpetuated through the transmission of values. Values transmission is necessary for community survival.

CHAPTER ONE

My Own Roots in America

I come from the working class town of Windsor Locks in Northern Connecticut. With a population of about twelve thousand, Windsor Locks was like many other small American towns in the 1960's and 1970's. My grandfather had been there since 1925. The town was originally the Pine Meadow district of Windsor, the oldest town in Connecticut and one of the first European settlements in New England. Windsor Locks was incorporated in 1854 with its new name taken from the "locks" that create a canal deep enough to allow commerce to flow through the shallow part of the Connecticut river just north of Windsor.

My brother Chris has been writing about the previously unknown Irish immigrant laborers that dug the vital Windsor Locks Canal in the early 1800's. As such canal laborers, the Irish immigrants were indirectly responsible for the economic growth of the Connecticut River Valley. These poor migrant workers were some of the earliest descendants of Windsor Locks whose relatives still live there with surnames like Costello, Fitzgerald, Fitzpatrick, Hayes, McMahon, McNeil, and O'Shea and to name a few.

Thanks to the Irish immigrant labor pool, Windsor Locks became an Irish-American town but at the same time also an Italian-American town, a French-American town, a Polish-American town, and to some extent a German-American town. Today's immigrants resemble those found in other parts of the United States as they hail from India and other Asian countries.

The opportunities for laborers to work at the factories and paper mills fueled the various waves of immigration in the past. Typical of growing American communities during this time, other jobs available were related to the transportation industry such as digging for canals, as mentioned above and laying railroad tracks. Subsequent to the completion of the canal, railroad service began in 1844 to connect Windsor Locks to Hartford, Connecticut and Springfield, Massachusetts. Transportation continues to be an important part of the Windsor Locks economy especially with the growth of the regional Hartford-Springfield airport known as Bradley International.

As the generations passed and the education levels of the immigrants' offspring increased, many of the descendants became professionals working in the Hartford insurance industry. Hartford is known as the "insurance capital of the world" and is only eleven miles from Windsor Locks. Many families in Windsor Locks could trace their lineage in this way, from immigrant laborer to professional. Some local folks still occupy working class jobs in the mills and factories that have survived despite mergers with foreign-based firms and the overall decline of manufacturing in America.

In Windsor Locks, the original groups of settlers were "clannish" to borrow a term my late grandfather often used. People were quite conscious of their ethnic, religious, political, or socioeconomic status. We took great pride in those identities and we were always aware of differences growing up in the 1960's and 1970's but also tolerant of others. There was a sense of community and national pride that bound us together despite those other differences. We loved our town and we loved our country.

Back then our small town existence seemed simpler than today. Summertime meant baseball, in one of many local parks. It meant the town pool, for swimming lessons when you were younger, then a place to hang out with your friends when you were older. By today's suburban standards, the Windsor Locks town pool would look small and inadequate. Nevertheless, to us as kids, it fit the bill. The water was wet and cool. That was all we needed, that and of course, the snacks stand. Every summer was also the Annual Fireman's parade and carnival. We looked forward to that event, along with the Strawberry Festival put on by St. Robert's Roman Catholic Church, one of two Roman Catholic parishes in Windsor Locks, which was the majority religion in town.

In addition to Roman Catholics, Windsor Locks was comprised of Congregationalists, Baptists, and various non-denominational faiths. Those from different faith traditions traveled to neighboring towns where resources could be pooled. Regardless of your faith in Windsor Locks, during the 1960's and 70's, pretty much everyone went to church somewhere and religious differences were not a problem. Kids grew up in neighborhoods that may have had German Lutherans and American Jewish families sharing a fence without a disagreement and developing lasting friendships.

There was however, one issue that could start a fight between local boys and between their fathers. The Hartford metro area, which encompasses Windsor Locks, lies halfway between New York and Boston creating a mixture of predominantly New York Yankees fans and Boston Red Sox fans. The intense dislike for the other team led to constant rivalry chatter among friends in my youth. Our schoolyards were filled with comparisons between Fenway Park's left field "Green Monster" and Yankee Stadium's "short porch" in right field. I would imagine those conversations continue today in Windsor Locks.

Neighborhood games pitted favorite players against one another. Other professional sports teams did not create as big a rivalry between two teams, although in football the Red Sox fans were probably Patriot fans and the Yankee fans probably chose one of the New York teams, either the Giants or the Jets to follow. Football did not have as deep a history of rivalry as baseball did in town. As for a professional team the entire town of Windsor Locks could jointly follow, the only one in existence was the Hartford Whalers ice hockey team, whose franchise folded eventually. Not until the late 1980's did a team the whole town could love begin to emerge as a dominant force. The Uconn Huskies, the flagship basketball program from the state University, united the state's disparate sports elements by winning championships. The town could finally agree on its favorite team.

Like all towns, Windsor Locks had its share of disagreements regarding town budgets and redevelopment that sometimes became divisive. The 1960's, 70's, and 80's were times of urban renewal. Historical buildings were not appreciated for their value, in this case, for telling the story of the town's famous one-sided Main Street. With the canals and train tracks on the riverside along with the factories, the storefronts were lined on only one side of Main Street. It was apparently deemed a better value to tear them down and start over with new mixed-use retail and residential buildings. Unfortunately, Main Street lost a lot of its charm along with its history in the process.

In Windsor Locks, most people voted, played by the rules, and participated in some way in civic life. In general, people worked together and cared about the community. Community cohesion and pride united us despite our differences. People in Windsor Locks were not afraid to express their loyalty to their community and to their country. They tended to trust the institutions that helped the community grow and prosper. Most of them were trying to live a good life. Windsor Locks people were profoundly moral people that expressed their morality simply. It was a good place to live.

Windsor Locks worked pretty well, although, along with the urban renewal, something else seemed to change in the 1970's. Like many communities in the 1970's, a malaise crept into the culture as the economy soured and positive feelings about the United States began to wane. The late 1960's and early 1970's had brought us Watergate, political assassinations, civil rights protests, and protests against the

Vietnam war. Many people grew more cynical and less ide-
alistic about America. Drug and alcohol abuse was an epidemic, a scourge that may still plague the community today.
There were vocal groups talking about remaking the country in a new image based on values that were presumably
more equitable and with more central planning from power
centers that were far from Windsor Locks. Small town people were degraded by cultural elites in the media as unen-
lightened, parochial, bigoted, or sexist, like Archie Bunker,
from the television show, *All in the Family*.

According to these self-appointed moral busy bodies,
everyone in America was supposed to be ashamed because
all of us were apparently responsible for the revisionist history that revealed how awful we had become or always
were but just did not know it. This was a turning point in
America, when political forces that had seized control of
the dominant narrative began to denigrate American people
from communities like Windsor Locks.

The attitude shifted again in the 1980's as the economy
recovered from the Carter dissatisfaction and Ronald Reagan
restored small town America community pride. My children
were born in the mid 1980's and benefited throughout their
childhood years from one of the greatest economic boons in
the history of the country that lasted from the Reagan revolution all the way until the bubble correction period of the late
2000's. Therefore, they have only known optimism and economic prosperity. The country had moved on and rejected
the cynicism of the 1970's. Even Democratic President Bill
Clinton had identified himself as a "New Democrat" and apparently discarded many of the progressive notions that had

dominated his party in the prior generation. It seemed we had turned a corner, back to liberty, neighborliness, personal responsibility and the belief in American exceptionalism, which were indeed the traditional values of the Conservative Democrat attitude in Windsor Locks.

The social discontent that was sown in the late 1960's never went away completely and has reappeared in this new era of fear and economic correction. Those same forces that told us how awful we were have shown up again, this time telling us our economic system is fundamentally flawed and a transformation is needed. They envision a new American system, more centralized, more regulated, more Marxist, more European, and less American. This revisited progressive critique is again threatening our core American identity, and this time it has the support of the President of the United States and much of Congress, although the 2010 Congressional election shifted the balance of power. I believe Progressivism is a fundamentally flawed idea that disrespects the American foundation. The solid majority of American citizens will beat back Progressivism again, and this time it will be gone forever, finally exposed as the imposter it is.

My family moved to Pennsylvania in 1991 in order for me to pursue post-graduate studies in family therapy at the East Coast birthplace of family therapy and one of the seats of American freedom, Philadelphia. We lived forty-five miles north of Philadelphia, in the rolling hills of a farming community that is known as the Indian Valley in remembrance of the Lenape Native Americans who originally settled there. The Indian Valley is made up of several small boroughs including Harleysville, Souderton, and Telford, is close to Lansdale, and not too far from the Allentown and Bethlehem area. It is also a short ride to Valley Forge, and only ninety minutes from the Amish Country in Lancaster County. The Indian Valley was a wonderful place to raise a family.

Pennsylvania Dutch families whose ancestors came mostly from Germany or Switzerland still predominantly occupy the valley. Perusing the phonebook, one would find a multitude of listings under the same name such as Alderfer, Benner, Clemens, Godshall, Kolb, Landis, Moyer, and Ruth, or some other recognizable Pennsylvania Dutch name. Initially, this made us a bit uncomfortable because we were not sure how well our family would fit into such an established community. We quickly learned that all was well because the local folks shared our core values, even if we had a few different traditions.

The predominant religion in the region was Mennonite, which evolved from the Anabaptist fellowship out of Switzerland. The Mennonite faith is the cornerstone of the community with variations in the area from the old order to the more modern branches. In addition, due to the German influence, the Lutheran faith was as ingrained here as the Catholic faith had been in the town of Windsor Locks. It seemed to us that there was a house of worship on every corner. As the years passed, the farmland continued to be swallowed up with housing developments to accommodate the influx of those escaping from the urban sprawl around Philadelphia. With the continued push out to country, the once rare Catholic churches found their parishes growing, which encouraged additions and new churches to be built, while the older parishes in the city began to close. At the same time, non-denominational mega churches also thrived in the area.

Over time, I began to see myself as an "Honorary Mennonite" because I worked at a Mennonite run company and treated so many Mennonite families in my practice in Souderton. It became fascinating to learn about local customs like F*asnacht Day*[5] and to frequent the local family businesses, which were ubiquitous in the area.

The Pennsylvania Dutch people are like many other groups that came to the United States in search of religious liberty. They found it in Pennsylvania, which had a rolling hill landscape that probably reminded them of their German or Swiss homeland. Like other groups of immigrants, these settlers found a way to maintain their own way of life while also accommodating to the American culture around them. As in all attempts at assimilation, this has not always been an easy process, but it seems to have worked pretty well for the people of the Indian Valley, who enjoy both the blessings of their own distinct heritage and the opportunities presented to them as United States citizens. The successful German and Swiss immigration and assimilation in Eastern Pennsylvania is an example of how well the American system has worked for over two centuries. This land of immigrants is held together by our common values, and is a place where people respect cultural differences.

Today I live in Portsmouth, New Hampshire, a town of about twenty thousand people, and a community that has the feel of a quaint European village. In my opinion, Portsmouth is one of the best towns in America in one of the unique states in America, New Hampshire, the *Live Free or Die State*. Portsmouth has a thriving local culture, a great business climate with an entrepreneurial spirit, terrific arts organizations, along with a reverence for history, tremendous local cuisine, an exceptional education system, and a citizenry that is empowered and engaged. Portsmouth is America at its finest.

This town reflects the way America is supposed to work. People act like neighbors in Portsmouth and they take responsibility for their community. There is also a radical freedom and growth mentality reflected by a thriving artisan and entrepreneurial spirit. This place is liberal in its political outlook and communitarian in its attitude. We may not agree with everyone here but we feel welcome in the community.

Portsmouth, New Hampshire reflects the best of New England too, that is a steadiness of habit and tradition amidst the exciting culture of perpetual growth and change. People are empowered and they use their empowerment to help others. The best example of that is when during the urban renewal period of the 1960's and 70's, rather than tearing down all of the historic old homes, the community stepped in to preserve them. People had long ago recognized the value of saving historic landmarks and renovating where possible to incorporate the history into the fabric of the community. Not everything was saved from demolition, but the majority of Portsmouth remains as a living, functioning museum.

New England and especially New Hampshire, more than anywhere else in the country, honors our essential American birthright of people in small, local communities governing themselves with limited interference from the state. People in small New England towns know community apathy and cynicism will bring about our demise because it will bring rise to statist interference like that which we are seeing in other parts of the country and all over the world. People here are good neighbors because they understand the alternative.

My frame of reference, therefore, is that communities can have diversity challenges but still thrive if people rejoice in their freedoms and buy in to the working system, which functions on the understanding that the whole is better than the sum of its parts. They also know that too much infringement on personal freedom in favor of collectivism leads to frustration, mediocrity, and eventually stagnation, which is a chronic condition that has emerged in many parts of the United States today. People in communities thrive and entire communities prosper when their citizens enjoy their freedoms and act responsibly.

Each of these communities, Windsor Locks, the Indian Valley, and Portsmouth, with their rich histories and Northeastern spirit, represent the best of America. They are not unlike many other excellent towns and cities throughout this great land whose citizens are doing their best to honor the American legacy of individual freedom and voluntary neighborliness. In Chapter Two, I will talk about some of those other places in the United States and throughout Europe, and some of the conclusions I drew from those experiences.

CHAPTER TWO

Freedom Around the World

During the past four years I have had the great pleasure to travel to forty states (allowing me to achieve the goal of visiting all fifty states in my lifetime), to all United States territories except American Samoa, and to ten countries on a spectacular adventure. I traveled due to my job but also in part to insert myself directly into different cultures in order to listen, learn, and share. It has been a whirlwind of cultural experiences.

I traveled to rural Alaska where I experienced what everyday life is like for the Native Yup'ik people in a five hundred person village that could only be visited by small plane or snow machine transportation. I took the plane. The village was plagued by alcoholism, suicide, and domestic violence, but it maintained a sense of ethnic solidarity that was grounded in their subsistence lifestyle. The locals blamed the white people, Russians and Americans, who had colonized them, for the problems they were experiencing in their communities. They were receiving a tremendous amount of federal funding that came with significant strings attached and limited their freedoms. This was in effect, a welfare existence that seemed to be made worse by well-intentioned outside intervention.

I worked for a time as a religious minority in a majority Latter Day Saints residential treatment center for children in beautiful Provo, Utah where I learned about the inspiring resiliency of Mormons in America. Mormons, perhaps more than any other people in the United States, deeply love their country. They believe Utah is the promised center of a promised land, The United States of America. Their struggle to get to Utah is legendary. In Utah, Mormons found the freedom to live their lives and practive their religion as they chose. Even though I believe aspects of their religious expression are in need of modernization I was impressed by the wonderful rituals and strong sense of family values I witnessed. Mormons have built a successful community and unlike many mainline religions in America, the Church of Jesus Christ of Latter Day Saints is growing.

I hiked throughout the Western United States, often by myself, meeting up with many interesting people on trails, in coffee shops and in brewpubs. The Western United States is truly the land of the free and home of the brave. The West was settled by freedom-loving rugged individualists, personalities that were quite different than the destructively entitled contemporary Americans. In America today, there is a yearning for this type of iconic American individualist, a yearning that is growing in this era of government interference.

I've been to blues, reggae, and Celtic festivals in at least ten states and tried some of the best beer in the world at some of the best festivals and the best brewpubs in the world including an authentic Bavarian starkbier festival in Munich, Germany. There is a distinct identity culture everywhere, which helps defined communities feel connected to the people around them. Culture is often expressed through food, drink, music, and ritual. People in communities all over the world fight hard when their distinctness is threatened.

I had candid sociopolitical conversations with strangers in places like Copenhagen, Denmark; Tilburg, Netherlands; London and East Anglia, England; and Stuttgart, Trier, Cologne, Hamburg, Munich, Frankfurt, and in smaller towns all over Germany. I believe there is a misconception about America and Americans that has primarily been fueled by envy and exacerbated by negative, guilt-ridden depictions of Americans in our own entertainment media. The fact that the United States is in effect still militarily occupying much of Europe continues to engender a love-hate relationship with the United States.

I had a chance to walk along Unter Den Linden in Berlin during a protest and see Hitler's bunker and Checkpoint Charlie, and later go to a place where part of the Berlin Wall still stands, talking with people who lived the East German Communist experience first-hand. Both of these examples of statism, Nazism and Communism, prove what can happen when the narcissistic and controlling impulses of men are empowered. The victim narratives in each of these situations overwhelmed good sense and opened the door to totalitarianism. Each system promises perfection but ultimately delivers tyranny.

I went to several traditional Chamorro barbecues on the island of Guam and experienced what lovely and generous people they are. I learned that the Chamorro people, the native people of Guam, had been colonized twice in their glorious past, first by Spain and then by Japan, and their native language had morphed into a combination of those two influences in addition to English. Today, Guam is like a welfare state where according to the locals themselves, people have become dependent on federal dollars and thus they have low motivation to innovate or to engage in self-determination. Most native Chamorro people are either working in government jobs or at one of the two United States military bases on the island. It is seen as lower class to work in tourism. Like in rural Alaska, unfortunately, alcoholism and domestic violence is common in the island culture of Guam.

Also while in the Mariana Islands, I visited many World War II sites including the famous *suicide cliff* where hundreds of Japanese soldiers and their families jumped to their deaths near the end of World War II. In the Pacific War, the United States lost thousands of its young men in order to reclaim its territories and liberate the inhabitants of the Pacific Islands from the brutal Japanese. As in Hitler's Germany, the rise of Imperial Japan was a sober example of malignant human narcissism, and the belief that it is possible to perfect the world through consolidation of government power and empire building. It never works.

I attended a traditional Hawaiian luau and was invited to dance with a beautiful Hawaiian girl on stage on my birthday. Today, there is a self-determination movement brewing in Hawaii that is suing the United States Government for reparations for what that movement believes was a violation of an 1893 executive agreement between the Kingdom of Hawaii and the United States Government.[1] This lawsuit is part of a self-determination movement that seeks to restore an authentic Hawaiian identity.

I observed union worker protests in Barcelona, Spain. Over the past several months those protests have grown throughout Europe as European countries are instituting serious austerity programs, much to the chagrin of the government unions and the services recipients that have come to depend on government largess. In France there was a recent protest when the government decided to propose raising the retirement age to sixty-two! We are starting to see civil unrest in the United States too as municipalities are beginning to cut back on services, jobs, salaries, and benefits. Most observers believe these protests will intensify as austerity measures increase. That day of reckoning is coming soon.

I attended Fasching (pre Lenten, aka Mardi Gras) festivals all over Western Germany and even a community Fasching parade in Chur, Switzerland. These festivals have deep and enduring pagan meaning for communities all over Western Europe. They are a living testament to the way people cling to the familiarity of their ancient rituals even in a post-modern world.

I ate tortellini, mortadella, and tagliatelle in Bologna, Italy and walked through an area of that city that was governed by a Communist council. Later I visited Venice and Milan. The people in Bologna, Milan, and Venice were unfriendly and aggressive and there were pushy street beggars everywhere. I had expected something different.

I got lost in Normandy, France and experienced good ole French hospitality before being overwhelmed by the sense of gratitude I felt when I visited the memorial at Omaha Beach. It was a serene day in May 2009 shortly before the 65th anniversary of D-Day was observed. The names on the gravestones were names I recognized and it reminded me of being in the presence of guys like that as a youth in my home town, Windsor Locks. America sent its best to liberate Europe from fascism. The United States, Canada, and Britain sacrificed thousands of men for freedom because had fascism won out in Europe, it surely would have spread. As a result of that mid-century crisis, the United States continues to occupy much of Europe today. There are dozens of American military bases throughout Europe, providing for the common defense but also contributing to the economies of the host countries. America continues to invest much of its treasure defending Europe.

I attended a festival in Belgium holding some revealing conversations with locals about culture and change. While there I saw a protest from citizens of Catalonia, who were continuing their centuries long quest for Catalan independence from Spain and France. It inspired and amazed me that people could cling so stridently to ethnocentrism. People want the freedom to self-identify and to determine their own destiny. Political factions, in this case Socialist forces, often seek to exploit ethnocentrism for power.

One of the most meaningful experiences I had was a trip to the Dachau concentration camp near Munich, Germany. I was struck by the utter depravity of course, but also frightened when I learned of the eerie similarities between then and now. The victim politics that resulted from the world-wide economic depression of the 1930's led to scapegoating and rage in response to helplessness, which ultimately paved the way for the power play of a charismatic leader. That leader exploited those factors in order to aggrandize his ego and assume totalitarian control, which is a real potential today under the administration in Washington, that apparently sees itself as righteous and more enlightened than average Americans. I believe the United States is moving away from its foundational libertarian roots toward incremental progressive authoritarianism. This is a pattern we have seen before and it must be disrupted. That sober experience at Dachau Concentration Camp accelerated the writing of this book because I believe our liberty is at risk.

Finally, I have had the great pleasure to work as a consultant for the past two years to support military service members and their families at bases around the world. I had no prior experience with military culture and found it to be a great honor to be with them, as they go about their jobs defending our country and advancing freedom. As the saying goes, *Freedom is not free* and our military families have sustained the greatest cost.

This is an incredible world. I feel privileged to have been able to see some of the most beautiful places on Earth and meet such interesting people. As a friend said to me one time immersing oneself in other cultures is a great way to learn from others while solidifying one's own core beliefs. I had a chance to notice the similarities and differences among peoples throughout the vast humanity we call earth and to strengthen my own core beliefs about human nature and the elements of healthy communities.

What stands out as important, as I think about what I learned about people from around the world, their cultures, and myself? People crave **freedom** and they thrive when they have it. People want to be **responsible** for their own lives. Too much well-intentioned interference from outsiders is character killing and causes resentment. The happiest people were the ones living in harmony with their **neighbors** without too much external control over their lives. People thrive in a climate of **thrift** and economic security.

When we start to believe there is a preferred state that man can create to make life perfect for the whole world and we go about imposing that master plan we are out of alignment with the laws of nature. Man thrives when he is free, self-reliant, connected with people he chooses to love, and economically self-sufficient. As culture change agents our best hope for success is to advocate persuasively for freedom and self-determination and model these enduring universal values as we cross paths with others.

CHAPTER THREE

The Civil Society

I recently celebrated my fiftieth birthday. The older I get the more I have come to appreciate the beautiful legacy of the United States of America that was left by prior generations of Americans to the citizens of my generation. Unfortunately, we Americans are on the verge of squandering what we had because we have allowed too much centralized control over our lives from government and corporations, which has contributed to a condition where there is too much entitlement. We have become self-centered, conspicuous consumers rather than interdependent and thrifty neighbors.

In the early 1960's, community and national pride outpaced any of the otherwise divisive attitudes that became more prominent in the late 1960's and 1970's and continue among many Americans today. The two decades after World War II leading up to this era were largely a time of optimism, prosperity, gratitude and patriotism. The threat of Soviet Communism created lingering fear but solidified the belief in the American way of life, as there was a sharp contrast between freedom and totalitarianism that most Americans easily understood. When fascism was defeated in Europe and

Asia in 1945 and the United States had finally recovered from its decade long Great Depression, Americans had regained a sense of comfort with the essential small town American values most Americans believed made the United States an exceptional nation. These two post-war decades were the prosperous childhood years of the first Baby-Boomers, who would become the most populous and controversial generation in American history.

Everything changed in the 1960's when the first Baby-Boomers became adolescents and young adults. It was during that turbulent period, the age of disillusionment that dramatic counter-cultural forces emerged in an effort to deconstruct the small town community values that held America together. A powerful twentieth century "Progressive" narrative was reinvigorated that was cynical about America and highlighted divisions over similarities.[1] The progressive position was essentially that wealthy Capitalists were subjugating persons with less means and had created a society that benefited only a small group of aristocrats. Progressives believed societies could be perfected. This is a point of view that came to America in the early part of the twentieth century and reached its pinnacle during the Great Depression when Americans were so fearful that they accepted all sorts of federal intrusion into their lives in exchange for perceived financial security.

In the 1960's and 70's Progressive forces that had made inroads but had largely been unsuccessful in the economic realm earlier in the century, merged their energies with cultural Marxists who advanced the victim narrative that drives the contemporary Progressive Movement in America today.[2] Marxist revolutionaries, who were mainly in our universities and labor unions, and spread throughout other institutions, exploited the resentments of African-Americans, other minorities, and women to disrupt the social fabric that held America together. The victim narrative overlapped with what some have called the hippie narrative that was nominally about peace but in reality contained advocacy for social and economic justice, which are fundamental Marxist tenets.[3]

These combined narratives rejected much of what is good about the United States and put forward the idea that the United States was an illegitimate country that existed only because powerful people had historically victimized others. The victim narrative was a deliberate political attempt by cultural Marxists to empower certain interest groups by marginalizing other more established groups. Their primary target was white bourgeois society, which Marxists, Anarchists, and Progressives believed was responsible for the subjugation of other groups and was therefore imperialist and illegitimate.[4] These leftist radicals exploited the anti-war sentiment of the time and legitimate freedom narratives like the civil rights movement and Classical feminism to deconstruct much of the fundamental American fabric. America has never completely recovered.

The United States is an imperfect union that was founded on enlightened principles, primary of which is the concept of the social contract, which maintained for the first time that average people had the capacity to govern themselves and could willingly come together to form a state.[5] Self-governance requires subsuming raw freedom, which the Founders believed was a natural right, to the needs of the community but it also requires vigilance against the inevitable controlling

tendencies and narcissism of man that would exploit government power. In governmental systems throughout history,
a man's surrendering of his freedom always leads to more
centralized control, corruption, and a diminishment of individual liberties over time. The Founders knew this tendency
and in their effort to create a well-balanced republic for the
good of all that also protected individuals, they carefully con-
structed a system that had safeguards against tyranny.

Our wonderful American experiment offered something
new, an idea that the people are sovereign and capable of
governing themselves. The Founders had enough foresight
and courage to codify that inalienable but fragile right into
our Constitution.

Thomas Jefferson believed for instance, that our country should be in a continuous state of reinvention in order
to deconstruct what he considered an inevitable controlling
tendency.[6] I interpret Jefferson as advocating a deconstruc-
tionist reform mentality every couple of decades to unwind
the inevitable build-up of man-made entrenched institutional bureaucracy. Jefferson believed such a reform is a natural
right of man. I believe we are exercising that right today in
the face of a build-up of government and corporate excess
that would have made Jefferson cringe. According to a recent Rasmussen Reports poll, nearly half of Americans today see government as a threat to individual rights.[7]

In the classic, *Democracy in America*, Alexis de Tocqueville
wrote,

> "A man's admiration for absolute government is pro-
> portionate to the contempt he feels for those around
> him."

Tocqueville anticipated the United States could follow the same path as other republics had in the past if it was not vigilant about its democratic ideals. Tocqueville revered America for its decentralized locus of power but he believed over time, people tend to gravitate toward more centralized control that props up powerful people who in turn exclude others from the opportunity for success. Tocqueville believed that, without eternal vigilance, that outcome was likely in the United States.

His native France, with a much longer history, was already an inefficient bureaucratic government in the 1830's when Tocqueville wrote his famous volume after traveling around the United States. However, since the United States had such a conspicuous beginning and was a product of the age of reason there were few other models from which to draw in order to predict how our democratic process might unfold. It remains to be seen if the evolution Tocqueville envisioned would fully materialize but many observers believe the die is cast if the current condition in America does not change substantially.

The current precarious condition is that huge expansions and consolidations in government and its sponsored institutions and symbiotic corporate mega-institutions with corrupt oligarchs are infringing on our individual freedoms such that many people no longer believe they have any control over their lives. This is a century long expansion that increased dramatically during the last four decades as an ill-informed American population bought in to the misguided progressive government fantasy that has promised a lot and delivered little. Progressives always speak up for the little guy but when they get power, they often use government resources to enrich themselves, their apparatchiks, and their wealthy friends. In the current reform-minded climate, that fantasy is being fully exposed and rejected, as only about twenty one percent of American citizens today believe that government is working on their behalf.[8] A majority of us believes we have lost our way as a nation and many of us are increasingly motivated to do something about it.

I consider myself a participant in the bubble-up citizen movement to restore America to its Constitutional roots in the tradition of Jeffersonian deconstruction. As a community builder and family therapist I have been working in the trenches for twenty years, one person, one family, one organization, and one community at a time as a voice for the restoration of the American community. This book is a continuation of that effort.

That effort is best associated with the political designation, Classical Liberalism, which is a close relative of Conservative Populism, although political scientists disagree on the precise meanings and origins of these terms.[9] I try to capture the essence of Classical Liberalism/Conservative Populism in our philosophy statement for *A Place for Possibilities:*

- We believe America is a country of boundless opportunity.
- The authors of the Declaration of Independence wrote: "... that all men are created equal, that they are endowed by their Creator with certain unalienable rights, that among these are life, liberty and the pursuit of happiness. That to secure these rights, gov-

ernments are instituted among men, deriving their just powers from the consent of the governed."Thus, we believe free men and women have a right to pursue their dreams as they choose and free individuals, exercising their liberty and acting in concert with one another and with limited professional interference have the best chance to create healthy and prosperous communities.

- We believe unchecked central governments eventually give in to the controlling and narcissistic impulses of man so we believe America should be in a constant state of decentralization, deconstruction, and restoration.

- We believe a limited central government has a right to manage institutions erected for the common good, in order to provide for the common defense and to protect the rights guaranteed in the U.S. Constitution, and only those rights guaranteed by the Constitution.

- We believe individuals are happier and communities prosper when individuals embrace both their rights and their responsibilities as good citizens and good neighbors, and thus we believe in the concept of ordered liberty, which demands that in a free society there must also be a vibrant civil society that promotes voluntary personal responsibility, neighborliness, and thrift.

CHAPTER FOUR

Deism Revisited

As a Deist, I am comfortable using spiritual terms like *creator* and *grace* but I do not believe the notion of natural rights is necessarily confined to the Christian religion realm.[1] Any person, regardless of his particular spiritual orientation, who applies reason to explain the universe, can embrace the notion of natural rights, as our Founders understood them.

As far as we can tell from the historical record, even though there were differences of opinion about the nature of Deity, without exception, all of the Founders believed our rights came from God and there was indeed an intelligent design to the universe.[2] Furthermore, as John Adams said, and this is a critical point many people do not understand, "Our Constitution was made only for a moral and religious people. It is wholly inadequate to the government of any other."[3] The belief in natural rights and by extension, *Nature's God*, is inseparable to the identity of our Constitutional Republic.

The logical extension of this self-evident Truth as envisioned by the Founders is that liberty cannot thrive among immorality. If people do not have the capacity or the inclination to exercise self-restraint and to be good neighbors, there can be no constitutional republic. The republic literally falls apart. That is where we are today. The way to destroy a constitutional republic like the United States is to weaken the morality of its citizens in order to make liberty impossible.

Many of the American Founders were Freemasons and/or Unitarians, or some combination of the two and depending on how historians have interpreted those labels.[4] They held the consummate Deistic belief in the existence of God. Many eschewed revealed religions and what they considered false claims at divinity and supernaturalism. However, their belief in God was essential to their vision for the new republic. That belief is described in the following passage from Thomas Jefferson, *The Existence of Deity/God*.[5]

"I hold (without appeal to revelation) that when we take a view of the universe, in all its parts, general or particular, it is impossible for the human mind not to perceive and feel a conviction of design, consummate skill, and indefinite power in every atom of its composition... ...it is impossible I say, for the human mind not to believe that there is in all this design, cause and effect up to an ultimate cause, a fabricator of all things from matter and motion, their preserver and regulator while permitted to exist in their present forms, and their regeneration into new and other forms. We see too, evident proofs of the necessity of a superintending power to maintain the universe in its course and order..."

Other writings from Jefferson also appeared to reinforce the notion that he believed in Nature's God and the
final judgment by God. However, even though Jefferson believed that the teachings of Jesus Christ epitomized all that
was right and good for mankind, he rejected the Christian
Bible as literal divine revelation and he did not believe in the
divinity of Jesus.[6]

Other Founders like Samuel Adams and Patrick Henry
were strong Christians.[7] Regardless of their beliefs about the
origins of these enlightened principles what they all shared
in common was their belief that the principles were part of
nature's law. The principles were larger than man and therefore not subject to man's invention or revision. Moreover,
the Founders believed in applying reason in order to discover natural laws.

I advocate the advancement of what I believe are universal Truths contained in wisdom traditions everywhere, inscribed in our Declaration of Independence and
Constitution, because I believe they are bedrock principles
that build healthy communities. I do not believe it is necessary to be a religious person or even to believe in a revealed
God to advocate for these principles. What is important is
that one have a belief that there is something transcendent
in the universe that is beyond man's control. We have the
power to change our world by using our reason to get closer
to what is true but we do not have the power or the wisdom
to invent new universal Truths or universal rights. Many
Americans choose to believe in God as the origin of Truth
and natural law. However, I believe it is possible to see Truth
itself as equivalent to Nature's God.

This is how I talk about my own spiritual beliefs:

Deism means there is something powerful and grand in the universe that is bigger than human beings are. It is larger than our ego's projection. Experiencing the Deity, how ever one does that (for me it is often being in the state of awe) diminishes our own tendencies toward narcissism and our controlling instincts. It helps us see order in things and brings peace. Deism motivates us to do good things out of respect for that amazing order. It also humbles us.

My interpretation of Deism leads me to be rational in how I explain the world but I am also open to other ways of knowing, such as emotional experience, intuition, archetypal awareness, or social intelligence. I claim no superior wisdom or privileged knowledge and seek to learn continuously from others. I do not admonish revealed religion or atheism but I do point out where I have reasonable interpretations that may be inconsistent with tenets of those other beliefs. Most importantly, I strive to approach life with realistic optimism and hope because I experience the wonder and the order of the universe.

While I am clear about my own spiritual beliefs and open to continuous learning, like Benjamin Franklin, who wrote these words below in a letter to an unknown recipient in 1757, I do not see any benefit in attempting to destroy organized religion.[8]

"I have read your Manuscript with some Attention. By the Arguments it contains against the Doctrine of a particular Providence, tho' you allow a general Providence, you strike at the Foundation of all Religion: For without the Belief of a Providence that takes Cognizance of, guards and guides and may favour particular Persons, there is no Motive to Worship a Deity, to fear its Displeasure, or to pray for its Protection. I will not enter into any Discussion of your Principles, tho' you seem to desire it; At present I shall only give you my Opinion that tho' your Reasonings are subtle, and may prevail with some Readers, you will not succeed so as to change the general Sentiments of Mankind on that Subject, and the Consequence of printing this Piece will be a great deal of Odium drawn upon your self, Mischief to you and no Benefit to others. He that spits against the Wind spits in his own Face. But were you to succeed, do you imagine any Good would be done by it? .... I would advise you therefore not to attempt unchaining the Tyger, but to burn this Piece before it is seen by any other Person, whereby you will save yourself a great deal of Mortification from the Enemies it may raise against you, and perhaps a good deal of Regret and Repentance. If Men are so wicked as we now see them with Religion what would they be if without it? I intend this Letter itself as a Proof of my Friendship....

What Franklin seemed to be saying is that even though there were components of revealed religion that both men probably agreed were unhelpful and limited man's potential, most men relied on specific faith in order to manage their impulses and to motivate them to do good things.

Furthermore, communities relied heavily on the faith in God and the structure of organized religion to socialize their citizens (as they still do today). Consequently, Franklin saw no benefit and indeed much potential harm to mankind in destroying organized revealed religion. For Franklin, as the passage above reveals, a world without any religion would be more dangerous than a world dominated by revealed religion. I am with Benjamin Franklin.

In communities where there is high religiosity, community connectivity tends to be better and people have better self-control than in areas that report less religiosity.[9] In addition, people who hold religious views tend to report better personal happiness than those that are more secular.[10] Religion tends to be a protective factor across socioeconomic and other statuses. Thus, even though some secular community builders might prefer a different interpretation, in my opinion, nihilism, or even hyper-rational atheism, pose greater threats to the civil society than religiosity. My hope is the version of Deism I am describing can offer a satisfactory middle ground worldview for secular Conservatives, traditional Liberals, and Communitarian Atheists who would like to join the American Restoration Movement.

Secular Progressives have abandoned the notion of God in America, and in the absence of an equally powerful truth narrative, they have also abandoned liberty. Without a powerful truth narrative (God) to guide human decision-making, the narcissistic and controlling instincts of man were empowered, which had the effect of favoring the illegitimate whims of charismatic personalities in government over freedom. One of the best examples of charismatic emptiness passing for Truth is today's Obamamania.

Recently I was hiking along the oceanfront near Rye, New Hampshire and came across a monument to the original colony in New Hampshire that was established in 1623. The inscription said, "So that God and liberty will reign forever." Liberty and God were inter-connected in the minds of the first settlers of this country. The early settlers believed God protected liberty and liberty protected the right to serve God.

When twentieth century Secular Progressives removed God from American identity, they also unwittingly removed liberty and personal responsibility; and created a vacuum. Many Americans, in their distaste for overt Christianity, have also allowed liberty and responsibility to be chipped away as government power has filled the vacuum. In my opinion, America needs another way to honor Truth without Christian evangelism so moderate thinkers who do not consider themselves biblical literalists can embrace the beauty of liberty and responsibility and other fundamental American values such as those I am advocating in this book. In this way, we would be returning to our earliest Deistic traditions, to the universal but non-sectarian spiritual notions advanced by our Founders.

While many secularists have abandoned God and replaced him with narcissism, there is a growing alternative spiritual movement in America that is attempting to honor Truth and wisdom. I believe this is an attempt by spiritual-seekers to rediscover the divine without what they perceive as the dogmatism of revealed religion. Many people have realized the emptiness of narcissism and are searching for meaning. There is a yearning for that which is true and good. This spiritual movement is primarily expressing itself in pagan or Eastern Ritualism and there are many such loosely defined expressions.

For many people, environmentalism is a pagan religion, which explains the intensity behind some environmental activism. Many such folks not only support environmental standards because they believe it is good to keep the environment clean, but they actually worship the environment as god. Consequently, to Pagan Environmental Spiritualists the environment demands more loyalty (worship) than the country or to any other representations of human organization because it is holier. Traditional Christians on the other hand would tend to honor the civil society and the people that uphold it as the primary source of spiritual energy and goodness on Earth. Christians believe people are the most significant of the inhabitants in the natural world that God has created for us.

Many contemporary Deists lean toward Pagan Environmental Spiritualism. My understanding is relationally oriented, which is consistent with the Deistic beliefs of the Founders, many of who were Unitarians who were closer to Christianity than to atheism, with Thomas Paine being the notable exception. I believe Paine went too far in his analysis.

Other related expressions like Wicca or Shamanism are also intimately tied to the earth itself as a source of spiritual energy. While I believe these alternative spiritual expressions are noteworthy attempts in the search for meaning,

I believe our Deistic Founders had the right idea and saw no reason to try to explain the unexplainable with new religious interpretations. I believe it is sufficient to recognize that there is something in the universe more powerful than man, which we can refer to as Nature's God, that started and maintains the laws of nature. Thus, man is miniscule by comparison and is wise to show deference to all that is around him.

This is a controversial idea during a time when people are tending to take sides. In polarized America, one is presumed to be for either religion or the state, which is the source of a tremendous amount of animosity. I believe one can honor Truth (Nature's God) without being a proponent of religion, which is the same unifying position that some of the Founding Fathers of the United States held. Truth leads one to natural rights and limited government, to freedom, personal responsibility, neighborliness, and thrift, without the need for membership in a revealed religion. Thus, there is plenty of room for religious, Deistic, and secular people in this American Restoration Movement.

CHAPTER FIVE

Societal Devolution

The United States is rapidly becoming a social welfare state like many European social democracies, which is a development our Founders would have strongly rejected. The Founders would have rejected a governing system that has citizens paying over fifty percent of their income to national income taxes as one finds in many European countries.[1] The taxes in turn fund a system, which pays for cradle to grave educational, medical, and social services. I believe they would have opposed a national healthcare system like in Britain that forces all citizens to get their healthcare through the National Health Service and government sponsored proxy institutions that answer to the NHS. Moreover, I believe they would have opposed a regulatory oversight system as in Germany that the local people say is so intransigent and oppressive that it comes with its own dialect, and squeezes out innovation and risk.[2] Each of these ideas, while popular today with many American Progressives, is decidedly un-American if one understands our core Constitutional identity.

Unfortunately, we are in the midst of a century long so-cietal devolution that accelerated in the 1960's and 70's as I mentioned earlier and has found renewed energy in the new Millennium under this current national government. Mischaracterized as progress, instead, what we have expe-rienced are the controlling tendencies and power of man masquerading as service provider and benevolent leader resulting in a civil society that is waning as social deviance increases.

In *God in the Dock: Essays on Theology and Ethics*, novelist C.S. Lewis warned us about the tyranny of whom he called moral busybodies:[3]

> "Of all Tyrannies, a tyranny exercised for the good of its victims may be the most oppressive. It may be better to live under robber barons than under om-nipotent moral busybodies. The robber barons cru-elty may sometimes sleep, his cupidity may at some point be satiated; but those who torment us for our own good will torment us without end, for they do so with the approval of their own conscience."

Americans have become destructively entitled, irre-sponsible, self-centered, entertainment-obsessed, corrupt, mentally ill, obese, greedy, consumerist, intemperate, and addicted as the evil bedfellows; corporate largesse and gov-ernment hegemony, threaten our core values. National iden-tity has taken a back seat to inclusiveness, while freedom is losing out to fairness. Over-consumption and greed have replaced thrift as core American values while our economy is in shambles with skyrocketing debt and no end in sight. Instead of refocusing America on our core values and offering the kind of sober leadership that we need to get out of this mess, our national leadership is doing just the opposite, encouraging more citizen consumption and more entitlement, while increasing government regulation and spending. Our government leadership and corporate interests are selfishly catering to their own special interests, which is perpetuating the problem rather than providing enduring solutions. We are in crisis.

This is how economist Bill Bonner sees the last several decades:[4]

"The boomer generation made a mess of the biggest success story in world history - the United States of America. In the '60s and '70s - when boomers matured and began to take over - the U.S. was still on top of the world. It had a positive trade balance... huge savings...massive investments abroad...and the strongest companies in the world. They ruined it. The financial industry took over...replacing manufacturing. Instead of making things we could sell at a profit, Wall Street sold debt - mostly to us! In government, imperial ambitions pushed aside the restraints and good sense of the old republic. ...... The sheep look to the government to solve every problem. Thirty-five million Americans - almost as many as the entire population of Spain, depend on the feds' food stamp program for their daily bread."

The function of Constitutional Republicanism in the new millennium has been degraded into a responsibility illegitimately given to the national government and American citizens through governmental proxy institutions to transfer money and goods from sources of wealth to other people both at home and abroad that have less. If we were true to our Classical Liberalism tradition, we would be using the divine grace that was discovered in Nature's God that underwrote our founding to be better neighbors by teaching each other how to fish and sharing the effects of our labor one individual, one family, or one community at a time. If most of us lived this way, we would not need expensive social programs or corporate consumer products and services that attempt to fill a moral failing.

As those government sponsored bureaucracies and controlling financial institutions have expanded in lock step with unchecked corporate empires, the psychological and physical health of the American citizenry has declined as I indicated above. My belief is that a deconstruction of those institutions and bureaucracies and a simultaneous diminishment of corporate influence will necessarily stimulate a return to the core American values of freedom, personal responsibility, neighborliness, and thrift. An intentional refocusing on these core American values will necessarily lead to a deconstruction of those antiquated and intrusive corporations, institutions and bureaucracies.

As I write this chapter, we are in the midst of the largest ecological disaster in American history, the Gulf Coast oil disaster. The disaster was apparently caused by corporate greed and inefficiency while influenced by government incompetence and bureaucratic impotence. It reflects wrongheaded institutional complexity and a tragic lack of leadership, which is fueled by defensive posturing because of the entitlement lawsuit culture we have allowed to flourish in the United States.

Fear of lawsuits influences practically every important decision made in American business and government today. My belief is the greatest threat to neighborliness and personal responsibility in America today is fear of lawsuits. When people are overly preoccupied with fear of lawsuits they become afraid to make decisions, or indeed to ever admit culpability by apologizing for anything. Without direct interpersonal responsibility and with the constant fear of making an honest mistake a community cannot thrive. Neighbors stop trusting each other. We face that condition today because we have allowed the legal system and lawyers to exert undue influence in America. I will talk about what I believe needs to be done to remedy this awful condition later in the book. Most of the other social problems that have infected America have to do with failures of personal responsibility and neighborliness. I will outline a few of these problems below, while recognizing that a full examination of these topics is beyond the scope if this book.

There is an emerging consensus among sociologists that the decline of the American family has been the greatest contributor to the disruption of the civil society in our communities.[5] Most scholars include: the rise in unwed pregnancy, single parenting, the decline in the overall marriage rate, fatherlessness, and the increase in divorce as under the umbrella of family decline and disruption. Each of these conditions has increased dramatically over the past four decades since the 1960's.[6] The increase in these interconnected social factors has eroded what was once the major primary socializing institution in America, the two-parent nuclear family. Not surprisingly, as the nuclear family has disintegrated in the United States, the civil society has crumbled.

Many children grow up without fathers and they are forced to endure the pain of divorce, both of which are risk factors for lack of educational achievement, crime, and the increased potential for their own divorce.[7] Single parenting and fatherlessness also have a multiplier effect as the problems they create often become multigenerational and therefore have a lasting affect on community health. This is particularly apparent in impoverished communities where the culture of fatherless and unwed parenting is intransigent and seen as the primary causal poverty factor.[8] The family disruption caused by fatherlessness and single parenting has had a profound effect on communities.

While the epidemic of teen pregnancy has received a lot of attention from Progressive grant-makers and researchers, many Conservative scholars point instead to unwed pregnancy as a greater risk factor for families and children.[9] The age of the mother appears to be less significant than whether or not there is a responsible father and husband in the household. The research shows that marriage has a powerful effect in connecting fathers to their children, both emotionally and financially. Women tend to be safer and do better economically in marriages than in cohabiting relationships. Children do better on a host of factors when they have a father that is married to their mother.

Marriage stability is an area that has finally begun to receive significant attention during the past fifteen years as a "marriage renaissance" has blossomed, but the emerging narrative risks being marginalized again under the current Executive Branch that is more politically sympathetic to a gender feminist agenda.[10] The protective potential of marriage itself had been insufficiently studied since the 1960's because the emerging consensus, that marriage has a powerful protective effect on men, women, and children is unpopular politically among the researcher class that has controlled the dominant narrative in the United States. Teen pregnancy, conversely, is a politically neutered term.

Some Progressive scholars argue the changing American family is merely in transition.[11] They see the American family as becoming more flexible and more responsive to the needs of individuals as gender roles change. I believe that is a preposterous notion that is attempting to justify the effects of a permissive society that is increasingly irresponsible and individualistic. It also reflects a shift in the priorities of many men and women who are choosing personal fulfillment over long-term commitment. By telling people that marriage was unrelated to child adjustment and adult happiness, Progressives gave permission for irresponsible behavior. The dramatic rise in divorce and single parenting that resulted from that permission giving has had devastating consequences for our communities. In my opinion, three decades of radical Gender feminism drove inadequate or biased research that disrupted family formation and marital longevity.

I have been concerned for as long as I have been practicing family therapy about the deterioration of essential masculine energy in American society. I call it the *Homer Simpson* Phenomenon, which is based on the character in the *Simpsons*, an animated television situation comedy and one of the most successful television programs of all time. *The Simpsons* is regarded as an important social commentary that takes a humorous peak into the absurdity and nihilism of contemporary American life.

Homer Simpson is a buffoonish fool who can barely get out of his own way. He is the family figurehead father who defers to his wife Marge, the power in the family, for everything, while Marge goes about her business of running the family. Homer's son Bart, a nihilistic smartass who occasionally shows glimpses of conscience but has the character of a hyena, is in and out of trouble continuously and never seems to grow older.

Without getting too deep into the social commentary about the Simpsons, my observation of the show is the way masculinity is depicted in the show is not that far from how many men behave in American families. Men are dead in America. In addition to becoming more prominent in business, politics, and practically every other aspect of life outside the family, women bring most of the new energy to families, make most of the decisions, pay the bills, and still have the lion's share of responsibility for the care and feeding of children.[12] Many men have deferred or disappeared from family life and surrendered almost all of their power to their wives, many of whom are wilting under the weight of all of those responsibilities. While there are some excep-tions to this rule, I have seen this pattern quite often in con-temporary families. The primary complainers are frequently women who want help but also want their husbands to stand up and be men, to assume leadership in the way that co-equal partners are expected to function.

The decline of the American family has coincided with an increased tendency for many to embrace an ethical sys-tem that sees self-expression as more important than self-control.[13] This is a troubling development because a civil society needs individual self-restraint and moral obligation to others in order to function. When community responsi-bility fades and narcissism grows, civilization perishes. As family commentator Bill Bennett opines in the above refer-enced 1993 piece from the Wall Street Journal, our society now places less value than before on moral obligation, less value on self-sacrifice, less value on social conformity and respectability, and less value on restraint in matters of physi-cal pleasure and sexuality. *If it feels good, do it* seems to have become the norm in decision-making. These trends have in-creased dramatically since the 1960's even in the presence of significant government intervention designed to address poverty and deviance. These broad cultural developments in our moral psychology place our civilization at risk.

Another factor that points to the moral decline in America is the proliferation of entertainment, sports and video games that many of our citizens rely on to fill their apparently empty lives. Viewing passive, popular entertain-ment has increased four-fold during the past forty years.[14] Ours has become an entertainment-obsessed culture. Much of the popular print or visual media entertainment reinforces aggressive, individualistic, and nihilistic behavior and does not give adequate support to traditional values such as integrity and commitment. However, as importantly, the sheer amount of time we are spending on these diversions is having an effect on productivity and intimate relationships.

Furthermore, there is now strong support for the existence of video game addiction, with the affliction affecting up to ten percent of all gamers.[15] It appears that millions of our young men are suffering from the same symptoms we see in drug addiction: social alienation, declining educational performance, sleep disorders, and inability to find joy outside of the gaming experience. This tragic development is further accentuating the performance divide between girls and boys.

We are witnessing a level of corruption in our television networks, magazines, and newspapers that has most people losing trust in traditional media and turning to the Internet for news. The most serious corruption in traditional media is the trend for media corporations to pair up with government to offer a propagandized message in order to gain dollars or favorable regulations. This is an example of political-corporate oligarchy.

Another disturbing trend is in the proliferation of "Liberal media" and "Conservative media." The resulting corruption comes in two forms.

Journalistic ethics demands that "hard" news be unbiased and according to many recent studies, it is not.[16] Hard and opinion news formats are increasingly being blurred together, which is confusing for many Americans. However, more disturbingly, many commentators in news outlets offer bias in one direction but do not disclose their allegiance to their audiences.[17] In my opinion, this tactic is primarily a progressive tendency, as the Conservative outlets tend to be more transparent in their advocacy. Either the Progressive establishment does not understand its own bias, which is possible, or it simply chooses to attempt to fool its audience, which would be unethical. These developments jeopardize the very existence of our Constitutional Republic because without an unbiased media there is no way to keep government from trampling on liberty. The Founders understood this well and thus took steps to guarantee a free press, which they understood to be a vital institution in a democratic republic.

Recently we learned about the *JournoList Listserv* scandal, an ethical controversy that offered evidence that the 2008 Presidential election was fraught with large-scale media corruption.[18] According to news reports, throughout the 2008 campaign there was collusion among Progressive journalists who put aside their journalistic ethical requirement for objectivity to conspire for ways to minimize any negative press for then Senator Obama and to find creative ways to go after the McCain campaign. According to the actual e-mails received from the archives of the listserv, known as JournoList, this collusion reached its peak during the scandal related to then Senator Obama's former pastor, Reverend Wright, and after Senator McCain nominated Sarah Palin for Vice President. This scandal is significant because the home networks and newspapers of these professionals promoted them as "straight" journalists, not opinion-makers. This appears to be a clear ethical violation that further blurs the line between propaganda and fact and is leading to record low levels of trust in the traditional media among the citizenry. Some commentators are lamenting developments like this scandal as indicative of the end of the objective press in America, which is a troubling if not fatal development for the country.

Another potentially fatal development is the obesity epidemic. Obesity is a sign that more and more people are eating excessively and exercising insufficiently. Most of us are simply eating too much of the wrong foods. Obesity is the greatest risk factor for a series of health problems including heart disease, diabetes, osteoarthritis, and high blood pressure. There may be a genetic component to obesity as there may also be with alcoholism and drug abuse, but many sociologists believe these trends suggest a failure of culture, spiritual emptiness, and a failure of personal responsibility.[19] Maintaining a healthy weight is a matter of consuming the amount of calories we need to balance the energy we expend, which is a simple recipe that unfortunately a growing percentage of Americans cannot seem to manage. Many people are coming to the sober conclusion that the obesity epidemic is the most visible sign that America has become fat and lazy, a sign of an empire that is in serious decline.

The tendency to demonize one's opponent in political conversations is another factor that points to moral decline. Our political conversations are increasingly resorting to name-calling and our media is capitalizing on the lack of civility for ratings. I do not believe polarization itself is problematic. I think it reflects a clash of values between Conservatives and Progressives in this country, a rhetorical civil war, which makes sense because there are diametrically, opposed worldviews reflected in the debate. The United States has been through many periods of polarization before and survived them. The most serious threat to the civil society in this polarized climate is the tendency of the Progressives to demonize Conservatives as racist, bigoted, sexist, or some other form of prejudice in order to stop the exchange of ideas. This political tactic avoids the content of the argument and destroys the opportunity for consensus building. More importantly, it destroys our humanity.

There is another troubling trend in America about which I can only offer anecdotal support that I believe points to the deterioration of our culture. It seems that Americans are becoming increasingly obsessed with animals and pets. Across the political and sociological continuum, it seems that many folks are creating an equivalency between animals and humans, almost to the point of animal worship. This concerns me and may point to the extreme fragmentation of society such that people are craving unconditional and nonjudgmental bonds, like that which can be received from a pet. It points to loneliness too, where people may be seeking out pets for social contact because they are not talking to their neighbors. A more troubling explanation for the animal obsession may be the devaluation of our own species, such that people believe there is no moral or spiritual difference between humans and other animals. To this writer, this phenomenon speaks to societal devolution. I am already anticipating a negative reaction to my hypothesis here; as a preemptive strike let me say, I do not hate dogs or cats!

Finally, as our excessive consumer spending indicates, many Americans have become conspicuous consumers who engage in wasteful consumption almost as sport. I will discuss conspicuous consumption when I write about thrift later in the book.

In the United States, since we do not have the totalitarian government structure as in places like China, or the pervasive shame-based sense of the expectation of adherence to community standards as in a country like Germany, or the dominant religiosity of our own Pilgrim heritage. Consequently, we have to rely on the family transmission and incorporation of voluntary individual responsibility and neighborliness to maintain our communities. Thus, these indicators of moral decline are serious threats to our American identity. Free people must behave responsibly or the free civilization our forefathers created will perish. That is a tall order in this era of societal devolution but it is our only hope for survival.

There are many people that have lost hope in the power of individual responsibility and believe we have become a terminal bunch of selfish sloths, incapable of self-control or self-governance. Maybe those folks are right. But I have hope – the hope that I am offering to my children, Lauren and Brian, that they and those from their generation will restore America by being carriers of the essential American values that I hold dear, freedom, personal responsibility, neighborliness, and thrift.

Offering hope and encouragement as I outline my understanding of these core values and the ways in which I believe Americans can rediscover them in order to produce

individual happiness and community wellbeing, is the focus of this book. The Republic is now in jeopardy because
of the aforementioned examples of societal devolution.
Consequently, our only choices, if we are to survive, are
re-moralization with deconstruction or increasing authoritarian statism.[20] What we decide as a people will ultimately
depend on who we believe we are or are becoming. Are we
for restoration or transformation?

Instead of evolution to a European style socialist democracy, many of which are near financial ruin today, I believe we
need a Jeffersonian deconstruction combined with a moral
re-awakening, a movement I do see brewing in the zeitgeist
albeit resisted by the expected power brokers from the institutional masters and their slaves among the citizenry.[21] It
may ultimately be the collapse of the dollar that forces the
societal deconstruction and community renewal but I have
hope that change can occur intentionally if a few courageous
leaders, with nothing to lose, step up and be bold. This is
one of the reasons I have chosen to write this book, to add
my voice to the growing chorus of Jeffersonian de-construc-
tors. If we allow the current trends to continue as so many
seem to be advocating, we are tragically surrendering the
time-honored principles of Classical Liberalism contained
in the hope of the American experiment. As Ronald Reagan
said, "If we lose freedom here, there is no place to escape to.
This is the last stand on Earth."[22]

CHAPTER SIX

Millennials to the Rescue

According to Neil Howe and William Strauss from their terrific 2000 book, *Millennials Rising, the Next Great Generation*, generational developmental theory holds that we are blessed with greatness every four generations. Like the Greatest Generation that saved freedom from tyranny four generations ago, according to Howe and Strauss, the latest generation to come of age, the Millennials, will be powerful change agents. Howe and Strauss believe the Millennials will depart from their more radical Baby-Boomer and Generation X parents and develop their own pragmatic approach to solving problems.

My wife, Karen, and I raised two of these Millennials with the expectation they have the power to offer something that can make a difference. Other parents in our cohort did the same, riding the waves of a growing economy and the optimism that comes from that energy to raise confident and high performing children. As of this writing, I believe the difference they can offer is a bit muddied because we are in a temporary political regression period but as these

Millennials begin to rediscover the Truth of the enlightenment and the American experiment, and the great promise of those ideals I believe they will find their power.

There is a false hope contained in the promise of what has been called Obamamania, which in my opinion is the latest repackaged progressive utopian fantasy, that will need to be dismantled to set the stage for the authentic American Restoration I am talking about here. I believe when the Millennials mature they will deliver us to a realistic promised land that will do justice to the profound aspirations, commitment, and courage of our Founders. In 2010, as I write this chapter, this perspective may seem counterintuitive or reactionary. However, I believe there are changing forces at play in the coming years that will set the stage for restoration and those emerging powerful forces will bring this hope to fruition.

Therefore, this book is a father's dream for his children. I do not share the belief held by a large majority of Americans who think today's children will be worse off than their parents.[1] As a realistic optimist and as someone who has already witnessed how special these young Millennials are I have no reason to believe they will not find a way to make the world an even better place.

I decided to write *Discovering Possibility* while I am still thriving and contributing rather than as a desperate old man's plea. As a coach, mentor, and teacher I still have some opportunity to influence and I am using that influence to attempt to change hearts and minds. We are living in consequential times and we need to act now.

This is a time of tremendous social upheaval, polarization, and economic pessimism. It is also an era in which our country placed great hope in a man, our President, who was supposed to deliver us from evil to a transformed place in which things were supposed to be much better. A lot of us believed his rhetoric was false and his hopes unrealistic. We did not believe the problems in America were simply a result of the effects of the prior eight years of President Bush's tenure, as was the ubiquitous refrain from so many Americans on the left of the political spectrum. We did not believe the internationalist, other-directed rhetoric that said America's problems were related to how she was increasingly being perceived negatively by the rest of the world. We believe our civilization is declining for the reasons I mentioned in the preceding chapter and we knew it would take sober leadership and big changes to get us back on track.

Every day I see examples of the utopian progressive fantasy being discredited. The impending economic and social collapse in Europe is the latest example of false hope being discredited and it helps many Americans see that big government social welfare solutions are not sustainable solutions for a thriving civilization. More Americans are also waking up to the divisiveness of the victim politics that are hoisted on us by the Progressive political establishment. They are seeing the inevitable result of that approach, which is people self-identifying as victims, and part of an ethnic, or other identity group rather than as Americans. President Obama is fueling that fire rather than offering a unifying presence in America and many Americans are finally waking up to and rejecting that divisive political tactic.

My belief is it will take a total and complete rejection of progressive hopes and aspirations to usher in a new acceptance of liberty and personal responsibility. A lot of us are working to bring about that disillusionment because we believe it is the only route to a renewed America and a better world. We believe the Truth is on our side and the other side is either in denial or simply craves power and will do whatever it takes to further an agenda, no matter how obscene history has proven that agenda to be.

Therefore, the Obama factor is the storm before the dawn. When more people wake up (and we do not know when that critical mass will hit), there will be a rush to enduring values and practices that are truly life sustaining and community enhancing. When the dust settles on this latest episode, our new Millennial leaders will be offered a more enduring foundation from which to re-build a better America. Their time is almost here.

PART TWO

Rediscovering Freedom, Personal Responsibility, Neighborliness, and Thrift

Foremost among the aforementioned principles and my focus in this book are the time-honored American values of freedom, personal responsibility, neighborliness, and thrift. For the purposes of this book, I want to offer the following definitions for the words I will be using to refer to those notions. Many writers use the terms *principles*, *values*, and *virtues* interchangeably but I would like to be more precise so the reader may gain a complete understanding of the concepts as I intend them.

Principles are abstract concepts we choose to adopt as guideposts for our lives. Virtues are community sustaining personal qualities that either we possess or we do not possess. Values are the things individual people or larger organizations appreciate the most. We choose to *value* some things over others.

Freedom, personal responsibility, neighborliness, and thrift can be seen as either *values* because they can be things we appreciate or as *virtues* because they can also be seen as

personal qualities that define our character. I can be someone that practices a thrifty lifestyle, for example, and I can
be someone from a family or community that advocates
thrift as a preferred way of being. Each of these notions is
also a *principle* because each reflects an abstract concept that
can be the focus of analysis. Therefore, depending on my
intention and focus I will attempt to apply the correct noun.
In most cases, I will apply the term *value* because I will be
advocating that we in the American community rediscover
and prioritize (value) certain notions over others.

In addition to talking about these American principles
in this book as a way to stimulate consciousness raising for
community renewal, I have also embedded them within the
mission of an educational nonprofit corporation, *A Place for
Possibilities* that has its home in Portsmouth, New Hampshire
but is a virtual, international organization (see Appendix). I
chose these four core principles after extensive research because I believe they are essential, distinctly, although not ex-
clusively American, values and they exist interdependent of
one another. In my opinion, the American community needs
to rediscover the value of each of these principles if it is to
survive and thrive without sliding into anarchy, which eventually leads to totalitarianism. It is not enough to advocate
freedom without responsibility or neighborliness because
freedom requires self-restraint and voluntary social conscience in an interdependent civilization. Thrift is the way
of life that ties the other three values together. Therefore,
I am advocating for a reinvigoration of freedom, personal
responsibility, neighborliness, and thrift as indeed the route
to restore a thriving America.

CHAPTER SEVEN

Freedom

The Webster dictionary defines *freedom* as "being free" and *free*, as "not under the control or power of another." As history proves repeatedly, freedom reflects the highest of all human aspirations.

Our Founders believed freedom was a natural right, meaning that it was guaranteed by God and was the basic condition under which all men should be allowed to live. The most basic belief, shared by most if not all of the Founding Fathers, was that men are entitled to be free and in the absence of legal safeguards, oppressive governments would enslave them. Thus, the birth of the United States was inextricably tied to the Founders' belief in man's right to be free and the vigilance with which the rule of law must protect that freedom.

All societies erect barriers to unchecked freedom. That response is a necessary and appropriate consequence of nurturing human relationships and building a society, as I indicated in my depiction of the social contract and ordered liberty in Chapter Two. Societies must account for freedom *and* responsibility in order to maintain communities.

In my field of family therapy, we believe the drive toward human relationship balances the drive for pure freedom, and thus, human organization seeks balance between these two fundamental human desires. People want and need three interdependent elements: independence, structure, and love. The question thus becomes, what is the optimal balance between pure freedom (anarchy) and social and psychological constraints. The psychological question thus supersedes the governance question, as the enlightenment philosophers well knew. They were pushing civilization away from religious and governmental repression, which had been the norm for centuries, and toward individual liberty, which made the age of reason an astoundingly liberal period in the history of the world.

The Founders believed we needed just enough restraint on liberty to sustain a central government but not too much restraint, so that tyranny would prevail. They were students of history who knew man's unchecked desire for power usually destroyed individual freedom, the same conclusion that Sigmund Freud later drew when he postulated his famous theory of libidinous energy.[1] They also knew too much constraint on freedom created repression, in the same way that Freud knew too much superego created psychological repression. Therefore, they created a system that attempted to balance freedom and control (ID and superego).[2]

Given their experience with the tyranny of the English Crown, the Founders were most concerned about vigilance against the inevitable tyranny that comes with unchecked power. Edmund Burke was perhaps the most specific when he wrote, "The only thing necessary for the triumph of evil is for good men to do nothing." And, "There is no safety for honest men except believing all possible evil of evil men."[3]

Thus, the Founders envisioned a society that was decentralized and barely beyond anarchy, giving the maximum opportunity for individual expression. They understood that human beings seek structure, and structure is part of free choice, but because of the controlling instincts of man and the corruption that power often provokes, they needed Constitutional protection against the threat of others imposing structure upon them. I believe their hope for freedom in America also mirrors the best recipe for human happiness on an individual level and that is what gives the idea its legitimacy.

I offer a blog for clients called Kevin's Korner that talks about ways to find more happiness and productivity.[4] This is a post from that blog:

> "The older I get the more I value freedom. It strikes me that most of the things that trouble people are connected to psychological or relational tyranny. That may sound like radical libertarian language but if you think about it, the happiest people we know are the freest. That does not mean you should jump on the next train to anarchy and dump all of your moral and social responsibilities. But it does mean that you have the right to live your life based primarily on your wants rather than your shoulds. Living this way allows one to choose his responsibilities and

relationships wisely to the extent he can, and avoid being an emotional pack-rat that comes from the tyranny of the incorporation of other-imposed requirements. Choose your responsibilities wisely and live freer and happier."

According to political theorist Hanna Fenichel Pitkin, liberty implies a system of rules, and a network of restraint and order, while freedom has a more general meaning, which ranges from an opposition to slavery to the absence of psychological or personal encumbrances.[5] In today's usage, the words are used interchangeably even though a more precise usage would probably bring about a renewed preference for liberty. Since I am focusing on psychological and sociological effects, I am choosing to use the more general term, freedom, but I do not wish to be disrespectful to the more precise notion of liberty, which has a stronger epistemological basis in American identity. Liberty is man's natural condition that our Founders believed was a universal right. Thus, the concept cannot be trivialized in the manner that the less specific word, freedom, often is in common discourse.

This psychological notion, that free people are happy people is not without real world evidence. If one looks around the world it is readily apparent that countries high on authoritarianism tend to be low on happiness and countries high on free choice tend to be high on happiness.[6] Furthermore, there is significant research to suggest that happiness is positively correlated with work schedule flexibility and personal control.[7] People that have control over what they do and when they do it tend to be happier than people who are on fixed schedules and with tight job requirements. The freedom to make one's own work schedule is an important happiness factor.

Communalism is not the opposite of freedom as some Radical Libertarians wrongly postulate. On the contrary, free people tend to choose to put energy into the relationships that matter to them and eschew those that are repressive. Forced charitible giving is frequently at odds with happiness. Free people also tend to be better neighbors because they are unencumbered by the resentment that often comes with forced neighborliness. Psychological freedom is thus, the antidote to an overactive Superego.

Free will allows us to live intentionally without emotional baggage, or as I like to label it, psychological tyranny. Psychological tyranny is when we allow things that haunt us from the past or fears about the future to disrupt our enjoyment of the present. Psychological freedom is letting go of those past or future tyrannies in order to experience the present fully. Psychological freedom produces the opportunity for happiness. Consequently, much of the work in psychotherapy is helping people learn to let go of psychological tyranny so they can make deliberate healthy choices.

A fulfilled life is an intentional life. The happy person is aware of his interdependence with his community and the opportunities it presents, adds positive energy to it, but does not let himself become entrapped by tyrannical darkness. Darkness usually comes in the form of narcissism, dependency, or attempts to control. Happy people make deliberate choices in order to experience the full breadth of humanity without getting engulfed by tyranny. A freedom mindset enables one to do so.

Thus, the real goal of all western influenced psychotherapies, in my opinion, is to help people discover the freedom to act on their own intentions, which involves, first clarifying those intentions and removing the barriers to the free expression thereof. Great therapists have faith in the power of individuals to decide what is best for them when they are free enough to act intentionally. The neurotic individual is constrained by controlling social introjects that overly inhibit free will and choice.[8]

Our Founders may not have been psychoanalysts but they understood this phenomenon well. Indeed they were operating from the same enlightened principles that eventually gave birth to the Analytic Movement that was itself a reformation against social tyranny. Free people can choose to act in ways that bring them happiness and can thusly share that happines in their neighborliness with their families and their communities. Forced neighborliness, conversely, is akin to martyrdom and often leads to resentment because the controlled individual feels he is a prisoner of other-imposed expectations. Consequently in societies where people are not free to choose neighborliness we often find pseudo-mutuality and despair. And when we limit choice we create powerlessness.[9]

It has been said that Americans are the most generous people on earth, a notion that is supported by the huge amounts of giving we do after natural disasters that occur around the world. But most of us do not want our government telling us how and when to give. We want to make those choices ourselves. We want to apply our free will to do good for others. This is of course a key distinction between Liberals and Conservatives in the United States. Liberals often advocate mandated giving in the form of taxation for the redistribution of wealth from those that have more to those that have less. Conservatives usually advocate for voluntary charity. In today's parlance this difference of perspectives is often couched in the social justice vs. voluntary charitible giving debate.

In a command system, even if the command elements are virtuous, free will is subservient to collective authority, which is authoritarian in nature. Man is not free to give. He is compelled to give in a manner that is reminiscent of how his mommy expected him to share his toys with his four-year old playmate. He does it but has no choice in the matter and derives pleasure only from the knowledge that he has pleased his mommy and thus will not be punished or abandoned. He enjoys no existential freedom or intrinsic satisfaction until he can decide for himself from his own volition whether he wants to share or not. Voluntary charity, thus, in contrast with coerced redistribution of one's resources, reflects an advanced psychological and moral stage of development.

If the importance of freedom is so intuitive and the social science supporting freedom so well articulated, why am I including it in a book written in 2010? Because not everyone agrees. Even after our Founders risked life and limb to fight for freedom and codified freedom into every aspect of our governance system there are still those that believe freedom is the enemy of fairness. They believe they must limit your freedom in order to create more fairness for other people, or for other creatures, or for the environment. They don't understand that their attempts to make the world more fair, even if well-intentioned, often have the effect of making the world more controlled, more regulated, less creative, and less enlightened. History repeats itself and we need to learn this lesson continuously, the lesson that Thomas Paine knew when he made his famous quote: "Those who expect to reap the blessings of freedom must, like men, undergo the fatigue of supporting it."[10]

CHAPTER EIGHT

Personal Responsibility

Personal responsibility means I am the master of my own destiny. It is the opposite of entitlement thinking that suggests others are responsible to make me happy. Free individuals are free precisely because they have taken responsibility for their own lives and let go of whatever primitive impulses they may have employed in the past to blame others for their own lack of happiness. The empowered individual does not let impediments get in the way of his own existential search for happiness, indeed he sees temporary obstacles as necessary challenges in the quest for meaning, flow, and the good life. He does not live in quiet desperation as Henry David Thoreau noted in his famous characterization of most men, but instead he desperately seeks his own happiness by taking responsibility without blame. He blames neither God nor man for his lack of success. He knows he is the master of his own destiny and he is up to the challenge.

This is a distinctly American attitude that is the overriding theme contained in the Declaration of Independence. Most Americans take this personal responsibility ethic for granted, but unfortunately there are growing numbers of people that no longer appreciate the self evidence of this fundamental Truth. This profound moral degradation is the great danger we are facing as a nation. An irresponsible people cannot be a successful people.

The prevailing new secular religion in Cool America is an adolescent fantasy and it has done great damage to us as a people. The guarantee of success without having earned it damages resilience and makes one soft. It also punishes real success, which creates an environment of mediocrity. In his excellent book, *The War on Success*, author Tommy Newberry offers the following powerful critique of socialist America:

> "For statists, above all else, things must be fair. In addition, by "things" they mean everything. In addition, by "fair", they do not mean equal opportunity or equal rules – they mean equal outcomes.
>
> The problem is life is naturally unfair. Liberty breeds inequality – when people are free, those who are smarter, better motivated, and harder working will achieve more than others. Therefore, the only way to ensure equal outcomes is to strangle liberty. In other words, the more government tries to make life fair, the less fair it becomes."[1]

The progressive political ideology, and indeed the overriding Marxist socio-economic philosophy that supports it, by definition, hold that people are motivated by their status as victims. Victim thinking and a sense of entitlement are built into those philosophies necessarily. A core tenet of

Marxism is that socio-cultural changes can only occur when enough people feel oppressed and finally revolt against the Capitalist ruling class that is seen to be the oppressor. Another way of saying this is the Marxist economic philosophy and all of its Neo-Marxist institutional extensions need people that experience themselves as victims for their programs to thrive. Marxist hustlers, as I refer to them, seek to make the population feel as powerless as possible and to eschew the concept of personal responsibility. If people are responsible for their own lives and are empowered to create their own opportunities for success, the Marxist narrative is destroyed. Consequently Marxist hustlers do what they can to advance the victim narrative, which is antithetical to the core American narratives of rugged individualism and personal responsibility.

Thus, promoting personal responsibility is the antidote to Marxism and is not only good for people psychologically, but it also creates healthier communities where people take responsibility for their actions and are better neighbors. The drip drip drip of Marxist thinking and Marxist institutionalization in America is insidious and destroys the character of the community by feeding entitlement and irresponsibility. If we are to restore the American community we must begin with a reinvigoration of personal responsibility at every level of society.

The most prominent institutions for the perpetuation of irresponsibility and the glorification of victim thinking in America today are associated with human services and education, the professions that are in the greatest need of reform in America. These professions are force-feeding this flawed thinking on unsuspecting victims starting at impressionable ages and continuously promoting their propoganda throughout the secondary and post-secondary American educational and human services systems. The culture of the human services and educational systems fosters an insidious groupthink that is at odds with a culture of personal responsibility. Purveyors of the dominant oppressor-focused political orthodoxy frequently attempt to smear those that would challenge their intellectual superiority. If you do not believe this is true, try speaking up for personal responsibility at a community meeting in a human services or educational setting and see what happens. Most likely you will be ignored or ridiculed.

According to David Horowitz, former 1960's era radical turned freedom fighter, the oppressor narrative in universities is most often found in our women's studies, humanities, english, human services, and social studies programs and is connected with a blame America belief system that holds the United States responsible for most of the problems in the world.[2] It sees Capitalism as evil and fosters a socialistic ethic for advancing civilization. These fields tend to be dominated by gender feminists who also believe the United States is a mysogenist country that needs to be reformed.[3] Gender feminists have been engaging in their revolution one student at a time for several decades. Often their reforms involve taking power away from men, the perceived villains, so that women, the perceived victims, can get more power in a society that not surprisingly, is becoming increasingly matriarchial.[4]

Gender feminism, as opposed to Classical feminism has alienated many men and women who wish for an honest debate about gender roles and gender differences instead of a war.[5] Instead of encouraging personal responsibility, gender feminists have often advocated using legal remedies to "level the playing field," which has had the effect of fostering an us vs. them climate in gender relations. Their misplaced notions about gender roles in America have created a cynical and self-loathing educated citizenry that actively advocates for social policies that are detrimental to the people of the United States. The enacted policies frequently exalt victimization and eschew personal responsibility. Many of us in the Conservative Movement believe the illegitimate promotion of Radical Gender feminism has come at the expense of healthy masculinity.

In my opinion, the Restoration Movement in the United States needs to focus significant attention on the human services and education systems, and particularly the specific disciplines in education I mentioned earlier. A new crop of realistic educators needs to offer an alternative narrative to Gender feminism, and other oppression naratives such as the alternative I am advocating here that is more realistic and less steeped in victim politics. It will take more than a value neutral position to undo the damage that has been done to personal responsibility and to our boys and girls for decades. It will take bold rhetoric and action. People will need to rediscover the Truth of the enlightenment, let go of societal guilt, and foster a new emphasis on personal responsibility without apology if we are to restore our country. I hope this book and my work as a community builder can have some positive influence in that regard.

As I write this chapter our world is in the midst of an economic crisis brought on by the bursting of a huge bubble that was created by a failure of personal responsibility at every level of society. The dominant media narrative, that I find depressing, is that evil corporations are preying on innocent citizens. The truth is that for decades, individual Americans, American businesspeople, and indeed much of the world believed they could have it all. Families, businesses, financial institutions, and governments lived well beyond their means in an easy credit fantasy world that eventually collapsed. Huge injections of new, make believe money in the form of "stimulus" are temporarily keeping the world economy out of depression but are saddling the Millennial Generation with a debt load from which it may never be able to recover – that is unless we act fast to restore prudence and sanity. Our leaders are giving us exactly what we do not need – so what else is new. A responsible people would take its medicine, regroup, and restore its character. Unfortunately we are not a responsible people because there are those that maintain political power by keeping people stuck. They are offering destructive false benevolence to unsuspecting recipients.

I believe personal responsibility and thrift are interconnected aspects of a healthy and prosperous life. Entitlement and spendthriftyness are interconnected characteristics of failed individuals, failed communities, and failed civilizations.

There is some good news as some European leaders and Canadians are seemingly rejecting the Keynsian theory of economics and adopting some serious austerity measures to cut spending in their entitlement based economies.[6] Great Britain and Canada are adopting as much as twenty-five percent reductions in government spending in order to forestall what their leaders believe could be economic collapse in their countries.[7] This is a sign that some world leaders are reconsidering the "have it all" mentality that has dominated western thinking for decades. It is a glimmer of hope in an otherwise destructive landscape. America seems to be lagging behind its more realistic allies, although if my premise in this book is correct, 2011 will be the beginning of a long period of economic austerity to the United States. A new day may be dawning.

CHAPTER NINE

Neighborliness

Neighborliness is the act of free people respecting and helping each other. It requires free will and conscious activity. Neighborliness is an economic, social, and spiritual concept. While neighborliness is sometimes conceptualized as a one-way effort it is by definition a social action because there is an actor and a receiver. Neighborliness is fundamentally a two-way exchange of services, goods, or positive energies between people exercising their free will for mutual benefit. The spiritual aspect of neighborliness is obvious. When that mutual exchange of goods or energies occurs, humanity benefits because each actor is improved and thus, in a better position to transmit positive energy elsewhere.

What are the psychological requirements and ramifications of neighborliness? Most importantly, one needs to embrace his own capacity to be helpful to others and he needs to be able to accept help from others. Each of these capacities is more difficult than it sounds because it opens one up for vulnerability. Giving and receiving are risky. So, being a neighbor requires a basic psychological centeredness that family therapist, Murray Bowen termed *differentiation* that protects the ego from too much anxiety.[1]

Often, folks that struggle with neighborliness are either fearful of abandonment or engulfment – being left behind or being smothered.[2] It takes a modicum of differentiation to be able to tolerate the closeness that neighborliness offers. Differentiation is also known as the psychological freedom to give and take without fear. So, given this definition, neighborliness is a social action that requires a psychological capacity.

Some people grow up in stable situations with well-differentiated parents that foster good differentiation and others are not so lucky. It takes some work for those in the latter group to develop a better capacity for neighborliness, and unfortunately, as an American community we are doing a poor job at helping folks develop this capacity in their daily interactions within the developmental landscape. So, it may take some intentionality for some people to build a better relational capacity. Those efforts to build stronger psychological muscles will pay dividends for individuals and communities.

Free people make healthy communities because they have an investment in creating the ordered liberty that will allow their families to thrive. They understand freedom can only be sustained if there is also neighborliness. This idea comes directly from the social contract theory that undergirded the birth of the American nation. Freedom without neighborliness is what sociologist Emile Durkheim referred to as anomie, the feeling of extreme normlessness, which many socialists and anarchists consider an evolutionary outcome of individualist free market Capitalism.[3] Americans know it is not inevitible that free societies get more and more atomized as long as their citizens are an ethical people who are capable of neighborliness.

America thrives because we have an acculturation process that ensures individual liberty *and* cross-cultural connectivity. Thus, one of the greatest dangers we are facing as a nation today is that our growing ethnic and cultural diversity will not also come with the requirement to embrace American notions of neighborliness. Without neighborliness we cannot enjoy the social connectivity that American communities need to flourish.

As Sociologist Robert Putnam points out, the more diverse a community is, the greater the challenges it faces.[4] According to Putnam, in more diverse communities people tend to vote less and volunteer less and there tends to be less civic engagement.

Therefore, the conventional wisdom, *diversity is our strength*, seems to be an incomplete notion that demands further investigation. This conventional wisdom may be true, but as Putnam points out there are greater challenges with diversity than we may want to acknowledge. Diversity presents significant challenges to social connectivity.

If one looks around the world he sees increasing division and strife as diversity increases, especially in places like Europe and the Middle East where religious and ethnic divisions are on the rise. America, which is one of the most ethnically diverse nations on earth, seems to be handling its diversity challenge about as well as anyone, a fact that our detractors around the world are loath to admit.[5] It may be that our traditional American notions of pluralism with voluntary neighborliness are thus underrated and essential elements for any society that wishes to overcome the challenges offered by growing ethnic and cultural diversity. We may have something to teach the world.

Neighborliness within does not necessarily mean Americans can not also be good global neighbors or that smaller enclaves can not also continue to rejoice in their distinctness. On the contrary, when folks know who they are and have pride in themselves and their immediate associations they also tend to be better citizens in the larger world. Solid core identity actually enhances inclusivity because the individual or the group does not need to prove his cultural integrity to himself and to outsiders. He is not afraid he will perish and therefore he does not strike out at challenges to his core. Neighborliness is really having enough confidence in oneself and in one's community so he can expose his beliefs to other ideas without fear of engulfment or annihilation.

In contrast with Europeans, Americans have always relied on the civil society to uphold the promise of the social contract by forming self-governing neighborhood associations. These associations were a means for involved neighbors to support each other and to simultaneously foster the interests of their families. Most Americans believe self interest and community interest go hand in hand although in recent years institutional power has begun to overwhelm natural supports in communities. This emerging condition is most apparent in our urban centers where blight and government interference are bedfellows, but it has recently

crept into our smaller communities too. Therefore, deconstruction and restoration will mean creating pathways for
more Americans to free themselves from professionalization
and institutionalization so as to (re)empower natural support systems.

One of the aspects of American life that destroys neighborliness is the perpetually expanding giant services sector of our economy, which is the fastest growing segment
of our overall economy. This is the central focus of one of
my favorite books, John McKnight's *The Careless Society*.[6]
McKnight makes the astute point that service providers
need an ever-increasing supply of clients in order to make
a living, and thus we have developed an economic system
that goes about *clientizing* citizens. Instead of seeking healthy
lifestyle solutions and neighborly charity from friends we
now tend to turn to professionals with the misguided hope
they will therapize, medicalize, or social work us to health.

While this idea has been around since Aristotle, in the
modern era this critique was most prominently put forward
by Ivan Illich, who like McKnight, believed industrialized
society was by its very function, causing deviance and illness.[7] Illich lamented the *counterproductivity of over-industri-
alized civilization* and believed over-institutionalization was
socially and culturally iatrogenic. He believed many institutions had become counterproductive to their original intent.
If industrial society was to rediscover healthier living, according to Illich, it would need to deconstruct institutional
systems and their reach so man could regain control over his
environment. Illich's words are especially meaningful today
as we look at a behemoth health and social services system

that is bankrupt and broken while the social, physical, and spiritual health of the population gets continually worse.

This understanding has created a lot of cognitive dissonance for me as a service provider as I have seen the way the American community has evolved toward a less healthy state to make room for our growing profession. The phrase for this phenomenon is social and cultural iatrogenesis – the proposed cure causes the illness. The incidence increase in depression, divorce, unwed parenting, and many other social maladies as the numbers in the services professions have grown, provides correlational evidence for social and cultural iatrogenesis.[8] McNight and Illich are right, that we professionals need clients to expand our monetary bases. This phenomenon presents an awful paradox that our nation needs to face.

Assuredly, efforts to deconstruct this iatrogenic helping system will be met with tremendous opposition from those that have a monetary stake in maintaining or growing the existing system. However, I believe if we were to deconstruct the human services system in America in order to create more simplicity, effectiveness, and efficiency, the health of the nation would improve dramatically. We offer an organization-specific transformation program to contribute to such a reform at A Place for Possibilities. [9] The current economic conditions in the United States may bring about a necessary deconstruction very soon.

Medicaid and Medicare are in crisis. This is how I wrote about their impending overhaul on June 8, 2010 on our blog, *Free Spirits for Truth and Common Sense:*[10]

"The human services sector of the American economy is the largest segment of the services sector, which is the largest sector of the American economy. Public human services are largely funded by Medicaid and to some extent Medicare, along with other public financing from government grants. Because the burst in the economic bubble that was driven by the obscene national debt is finally getting the attention it needs, the federal government will no longer have the political clout it needs to borrow or print money at will (although they will try for as long as they can). The Keynesian Economists, with their emphasis on "stimulus" spending, which so far has largely been in the form of continued payouts to services sector unions and other government stakeholders and friends, are losing the economic argument. Therefore, it appears that the federal government and many states will soon cut Medicaid funding.

The states, that are completely dependent on the fifty percent federal government match for all Medicaid dollars that is guaranteed by law, will be unable to continue services as usual, services that have increased dramatically during the bubble years. These cuts and associated shortfalls are happening right now. It will create a huge outcry from the usual cultural Marxist advocates who will claim the government is evil, unfair, and racist, even though the motivation for the outcry will not really be about client care but in reality, about the Medicaid created jobs, perks, and pensions that are in jeopardy when these funds are cut. If integrity prevails, the fiscal realists will win out and the funds will be cut in spite of the rage. If the government gives in again we will merely be pushing the problem a bit further down the road.

As this is happening in parts of Europe, it has lead to riots in the streets by government employee unions and Communists. Unfortunately, that same outcome is likely in the United States, although the overt Communist presence will be muted. But if we keep our heads, when the dust settles we will be left with a need for a new type of human services system that is more efficient, necessarily, and less reliant on government funding because there will be a lot less left to go around. What will that new system entail?

If my generation does not have the courage to do the right thing, Millennial leaders should immediately go about the business of intentionally defunding and deconstructing our behemoth human services system in order to improve the health of the nation. That step would renew neighborliness more than any other systemic action. Of course it would be met with tremendous opposition from stakeholders in that system so it will take real courage to get it done. The time is now. Unfortunately because my generation lacks courage, and politicians have been buying votes through that system for decades, and consequently many of us are feeding at the human services trough, it may take the full collapse of the economy to bring it about."

In addition to the reasons above there are a couple of other factors that have contributed to the dramatic shift toward a services economy. The increase in women relative to men in university enrollment and the corresponding rise of women in the professional workforce means there are growing numbers of workers who tend to gravitate to the helping professions.[11] And as that sector grows it needs to sustain itself with an ever-increasing supply of workers, most of whom are women. Conversely, as the working population of women grows, that group needs an ever-increasing supply of jobs. Most of the commentary on this social trend tends to be positive although I have seen few studies that have looked at the long term implications of this development and the effects it is sure to have on the services and manufacturing sectors of the economy respectively.

This development coincides with the demise of the manufacturing sector of our economy due to high labor costs and the inability to compete with third world developing economies like China. Therefore ours has become a professional services society with most of our great minds gravitating toward financial and social services instead of engineering and science. We are no longer making things people need but instead selling people our services. At the same time we are convincing people they need more and more of those services, which are themselves iatrogenic to community health and wellbeing. Professionalization is thus an inevitible by-product of prosperity but is paradoxically also destroying creativity and community as McNight and Illich postulated.

My intention is to contribute to the reversal of this several decades long trend as it not only skewed the landscape in favor of the feminine and put a lot of men out of work, but it has also disempowered neighborliness. Professional service providers are not neighbors. They are workers who are offering pseudo-kindness for money. Recipients understand the provider-user relationship is artificial and it leads to a lack of permanence and a kind of pseudomutuality in day to day relationships. Furthermore, the ubiquitousness of those professional relationships crowds out regular neigborliness, which gives people a real sense of connection and self-worth. Too much professionalism is thus anti-community.

A business associate is not a friend. He is a client. But many professional people are conflating the two and have few unencumbered relationships. This is creating an artificial society where people understand their relationships have dual purposes, which interferes with the human need for unconditional friendship. This phenomenon is also placing undue pressure on romantic relationships and marriages because in this artificial world of friendship people are asking for too much intimacy from their spouses. This has created a situation in which the American community is failing to meet the most basic needs of its members.

CHAPTER TEN

Thrift

Thrift is a nearly forgotten American virtue.

The following quote is from the excellent 2009 book, written by David Blankenhorn, Barbara Dafoe Whitehead, and Sorcha Brophy-Warren entitled, *Franklin's Thrift; The Lost History of An American Virtue.*

"For Benjamin Franklin, who personified and promoted the idea, thrift meant working productively, consuming wisely, saving proportionally, and giving generously. Franklin's thrift became the cornerstone of a new kind of secular faith in the ordinary person's capacity to shape his lot and fortune in life."

At almost fifteen trillion dollars per year, the economy of the United States is the largest economy in the world and consumer spending accounts for about seventy percent of our gross domestic product.[1] The exploding new economies in China and India are entirely dependent on Americans continuing to spend profusely, an economic partnership that unfortunately we are all too willing to embrace. Think about that. Three hundred million U.S. citizens are economically responsible for a world population of almost seven billion people. What would happen to the world economy if United States consumers cut back on their spending? Many Americans have come to believe that conspicuous spending is our patriotic duty, an absurd notion, but an unfortunate reality in these troubled times.

As we have seen recently during this global economic decline, when American citizens slow their spending all of the world's markets are affected and the entire global economic system is placed at risk. Some have called it *mutually assured economic destruction*, which means the United States has a symbiotic relationship with other economic powers.[2] The symbiotic relationship ensures homeostasis because of the knowledge that a change in one country would affect another, which would create a domino effect that could lead to the demise of everyone. A more linear way of stating this unfortunate reality is that most of the world relies on excessive American consumer spending so it can keep producing goods and services, and thus the American consumer and thrift have necessarily parted company. Living an unthrifty lifestyle is built into the world homeostatic condition, which is placing an undue burden on Americans.

As I write this paragraph, the United States just contributed to the bailout of Greece through the International Monetary Fund, to the tune of several hundred billion dollars, a contribution that seems almost unworldly, and a contribution that most Americans opposed.[3] Apparently, there may be more such bailouts in the near future along with the existing foreign aid commitments, which are already un-sustainable. We are spending money we do not even know about and money we have to borrow from other countries to spend! However, as I wrote earlier, there may be some hope on the horizon because a growing percentage of Americans is rejecting this unthrifty practice.

Our own federal spending on entitlement programs, military expansion, and wasteful bureaucracy is killing the national economy at large. As I write this, our country is running the highest monthly deficits of all time in adjusted for inflation numbers, many states are on the verge of bank-ruptcy because of out of control spending, and social pro-grams that have unsustainable future liabilities.[4] We have a financial mess on our hands.

Many American individuals and families are in serious financial trouble. Family debt relative to disposable income was at an all time high at the end of 2009.[5] Personal bank-ruptcies and housing foreclosures are also at all time highs while personal savings rates remain low (although savings rates have begun to climb in 2009-10 as more families are taking the steps necessary to balance their financial ledg-ers[6]). The credit card has become the preferred way to pur-chase goods and services; so most Americans no longer be-lieve reserve cash is a prerequisite to buying anything. *Buy now and pay later* has become the norm for many people. International spending and debt norms are mirroring what is happening on the individual and family level in the United States.[7]

Social psychology research indicates that people who hold a *materialistic value orientation* tend to score lower on scales that measure subjective wellbeing (happiness).[8] Moreover, since people who score high on materialism tend to be more anxious and more depressed than people who score low on materialism, it stands to reason that the excessive spending associated with a materialistic value orientation may be contributing to the depressogenic condition that is afflicting so many Americans today. If our goal is to create a culture that generates better happiness, we would be wise to evaluate Americans' spending attitudes and spending levels and create a renewed focus on thrift as a national priority. Maintaining a thrifty lifestyle is the antidote to living one's life with a materialistic value orientation.

Thrift is a lifestyle commitment that requires prudence, responsibility, and discipline, which are forgotten aspects of the American character. The thrifty lifestyle offered one an opportunity to earn success and build stability, two important aspects of community connectivity. Thrift allowed one to establish independence and to invest in the future while building relationships with one's neighbors. Being thrifty means one is living a life that embraces both receiving and giving, which are the basis of healthy psychological differentiation as I mentioned earlier. Therefore, while thrift is sometimes thought of as a minor virtue, in actuality it is the most comprehensive of all the American virtues I have talked about so far. Thrift is a complete concept.

Furthermore, some scholars are calling into question the conventional wisdom known as the *paradox of thrift*, attributed to economist, John Maynard Keynes.[9] The paradox of thrift concept contains the seemingly logical notion that one man's income is another man's savings. Keynes believed if one person stops spending, especially during an economic downturn, he/she is taking money away from another person whose income depends on the others' spending. Thrift thus becomes an unwanted individual activity because it presumably hurts others in the economy. The implication of the paradox of thrift is that a robust economy depends on high rates of spending by either individuals or governments. Consequently, in this way of thinking, thrift would be anathema to a healthy and growing capitalistic economy.

David Blankenhorn, President of the Institute for American Values, wrote the following in a *Weekly Standard* publication entitled: *There is no Paradox of Thrift.*[10]

> "Savers are actually likely to spend **more** than people mired in debt. Couples who practice thrift and build wealth over time have more assets and savings, which in turn become productive investments, which in turn promote economic growth and development. Such thrifty couples also tend to pay more taxes. This whole dynamic is good for families and for their society. In fact, if the goal is more stimulative spending, thrift is the main way to get there."

So, if we are to restore a more sober and prosperous America we would be wise to dismiss the notion of the paradox of thrift. Excessive spending may have some temporary benefit for producers but it has long term negative consequences for society.

During the past sixty years, the American psychology has shifted from thrift to self-actualization and individual creative expansionism. In my opinion, this accelerating individualistic/humanistic trend has been anti-community. For as thrift is a relational concept as Franklin explained, self-actualizing consumerism without communion fosters independence without relationship. Buying stuff makes people feel good temporarily but creates a world full of stuff that lacks meaning and purpose. In a more prosperous and sober community, individual creative expansionism as a quasi-religion would be replaced by thrift in the way Benjamin Franklin envisioned thrift over two hundred years ago.

We can see more evidence of the tendency of many Americans to turn from communion to self in a recent survey released by a group of scholars in the American Journal of Advertising Research.[11] These researchers found that *self-respect* has become the most important social value for Americans while *sense of belonging* has steadily declined since the 1970's. This is not a surprising finding, given as the authors of this study surmised, "If a person looks to him or herself as the ultimate arbiter of most things, a need for belonging ought to correspondingly diminish." People tend to be less concerned about what others think of them, which may have some advantages from a psychological standpoint but also supports the disturbing notion that people are becoming less community-minded. Consequently, many people are willing to spend a lot of money on education and other self-improvement and less on investment in community capital. For a culture of thrift to be reinvigorated in America, that individualistic trend would need to be reversed. Thrift requires both individual discipline and social responsibility.

The media/self-help/psychotherapy humanism of to-day teaches people they can have it all without having to be responsible for anything but themselves. Moreover, it tells people they should not deny themselves anything because a life of abundance magically seems to make everyone better simultaneously.

Credit is there to allow individuals to get whatever they want whenever they want it (although we are now in the midst of a rude awakening). Credit is a tool of self-actuali-zation. It has no end. The credit rationale is that the life of abundance should be available to everyone no matter one's station in life, or how hard he has worked, or how much self-discipline he has displayed. If instead we returned the national psyche to thrift instead of credit and consumption, we would have the real opportunity for community renewal.

PART THREE

The Hard Work of Restoring
the American Community

My belief that we have entered a restorative phase in our American existence comes from the awareness that the larger civilization is in crisis, which places civilization at the apex of opportunity. I believe the world has entered a new axial phase, a second great enlightenment period, which will lead to massive social change in a short time period.[1] Thus, I believe we are living in consequential times that will provide fertile ground for the rediscovery of the enlightened American notions I have been talking about in this book.

Conservatives are not typically community organizers so this battleground is foreign to most of the people to whom my message is intended. Community agitation and change has typically been the purview of people on the left. Since I do have a background in community mobilizing and culture change, I am trying to bring my expertise as an agent of change in many settings to the American Restoration

Movement. This is not a political campaign. It is a community renewal social movement. Consequently, we must approach change as social entrepreneurs and community mobilizers if we are to have a lasting effect.

My way of looking at community organizing is that it is a democratic process that attempts to build leaders who work through one relationship at a time to change a dominant narrative. Relationships can be either face to face, or virtually, through citizen blogging and Internet social networking. All communication mediums are vehicles for messaging. As the dominant narrative changes, the power centers that rely on the old narrative for legitimacy are deconstructed. Bubble-up local community organizing interacts with top-down and other media generated organizing in a dynamic, values-driven change process. The goal is to create sustained momentum around common sense conservative ideas in such a way that those ideas eventually become the preferred narrative. That is how a culture changes.

Social entrepreneurs use the principles of social marketing to foster ideas rather than products or services.[2] The goal of the American Restoration Movement is to use social marketing to foster the principles of Classical Liberalism, which I have delineated succinctly in this book as represented by the fundamental values: freedom, personal responsibility, neighborliness, and thrift. If Classical Liberalism can become the dominant socio-political narrative, it has the potential to overwhelm twentieth century Progressivism. This is our epic challenge and opportunity, and is the hard work of restoring the American community.

In the following sections, I will write about how I believe America is on the verge of a massive radical deconstruction and restoration. I will outline how I see the revival occurring and what steps we should take to solidify and accelerate the process.

CHAPTER ELEVEN

Free Spirits for Truth and Common Sense

How do we, Common Sense Conservatives contribute to the grass roots citizen movement to restore the American community?

Our tactic is using evangelism for Truth. We want to be both well differentiated and respectful and we especially want to reach people that are not often exposed to our message. This is what the American Restoration Movement is all about and there are many of us out here in the trenches fighting for Truth, and each doing what we can in our own spheres of influence to be carriers of that change energy. We are fighting some powerful and equally committed forces like the political Progressives, the social justice warriors, the gender feminists, the Marxists, the globalists, the cultural and moral relativists, the European Socialists, and many others who do not believe in Classical Liberalism. However, our numbers are growing and we believe we have the truth on our side. Therefore, we will stay the course until the restoration is complete, and the American community is restored to the original intention of the Founders. We see the process unfolding as below.

The Unfolding Process

I have written about how I believe individuals will be happier if they embrace freedom, personal responsibility, neighborliness, and thrift. More importantly, I believe our American communities will begin to prosper again when these principles return to the forefront of American life. In this chapter, I want to talk about ways that more people can rediscover these notions and how the community would organize itself differently to create more opportunities for the actualization of these values. As these values are embraced by more and more people, and particularly by people who have not previously been exposed to our American tradition, or previously had not seen themselves as connected to that tradition, I believe there will be a dramatic cultural shift in America. My hope is this book and our corresponding advocacy will inspire Common Sense Conservatives to continue to move forward with a tangible action plan in this important moment of opportunity. I also hope to convert others to join the growing Movement.

There are many excellent new conservative road maps for success in the political sphere, and many more being developed on a daily basis. These are consequential times in America and many people are activated. The Tea Party Movement is responsible for giving many of these plans energy, even in the midst of a powerful resistance from Socialist forces in America who are using their newly found power to stifle dissent. Most of these emerging plans are economic and structural because they are coming from the political class. My plan will contain economic and structural recommendations but it will also be directed at the ideological, moral, psychological, social, and spiritual realms that make up the core of who we are. A complete restoration is needed and this is the beginning.

My economic plan comes from the realization that the United States is already in a period that has been characterized by economist Bill Bonner as The Great Correction.[1] The economy had been in a bubble since the Reagan administration and that bubble has finally ended. This is good. Like all bubbles, it produced economic prosperity but also moral depravity. In this case, we have allowed government programs to grow to unsustainable levels and we have seen corporations and financial institutions running wild with greed. All economic corrections are important opportunities for spiritual correction too, and this one will be no different. These periods give us an opportunity to put our desires on a diet and to re-set our priorities. In this case, we need to deconstruct our seemingly insatiable and irresponsible empire and rediscover thrift and personal responsibility.

This week, Republicans gained control of the House of Representatives because the approval ratings for Democratic leaders in Congress and for President Obama remain abysmal. The people are stirred. I believe the results of the 2010 Congressional election indicate that we are witnessing a virulent grass roots restorative revolution like none other in the history of this country to undue the socialist advances that have occurred since 2008 and have been accumulating since the turn of the century.

Constitutional Conservatives have succeeded in attracting independent voters who may be less enamored with social conservatism but want to see our political leaders rediscover common sense. Another interesting result of the 2010 election is that some Republicans who were considered too religious or too all-or-nothing in their thinking lost. Thus, this is the time for the ascendancy of Common Sense Conservatism in America.

Conservatives on the airwaves have teamed up with grass roots citizen movements, using the new media to uncover the insidious socialist advances in the United States, a development that has aroused a counter-revolution in America that I have not seen in my lifetime. There is no stopping the counter-revolution because it is firmly grounded in Classical Liberalism and fueled by righteous anger. The election of a Progressive, *Post-American* President, Obama and his actions since elected are the impetus this quiet majority has needed to assert itself, and they will in the coming years.[2] Change will happen quickly.

Making America Cool Again

The most important thing we need to do is continue to use our rhetorical and electoral might to stop the political progressive onslaught that currently has momentum in this country and around the world. That agenda caught fire because many Americans were depressed about the war and the economy and a cool candidate came along to offer an interesting alternative, an alternative that in times of better clarity would appeal to only about fifteen to twenty percent of the U.S. population, the amount of U.S. citizens that identify themselves as liberal or very liberal.[3] In addition,

President Bush was unable to inspire a depressed silent majority of Americans to stay with his agenda, especially during the economic crisis that came at the end of his Presidency. Independents blamed Republicans, bankers, and Capitalists for the crisis (which was too narrow a lens) but it was a narrative that empowered the Progressive candidates who were positioning themselves as the Populist/anti-Capitalists. It was a perfect storm on the Conservative Movement that even in a center-right country, led to a huge change of power and allegiance in Washington.

Another factor that gets insufficient attention in my opinion is that the independent middle of the country, especially in Northern states and upper middle class neighborhoods throughout the country is rejecting in your face conservative religious fundamentalism and simultaneously attempting to maintain its common sense conservative ideals. A large majority of Americans still believes in God. Spiritual activism is on the rise, but many folks are tired of the all or nothing exclusion politics they perceive coming from people who espouse a worldview that excludes others from salvation. There is an especially pronounced stylistic divide, that is often unspoken, between Northern and Southern Conservatives, with the former group rejecting the fire and brimstone rhetoric of Southern conservatism while attempting to hold onto core Constitutional Conservative tenets. In my opinion, this is the primary reason there are very few Conservatives holding national electoral offices from the Northeastern United States, although that trend reversed during the most recent Congressional election in 2010. I know many people from the Northeast who are culturally and economically conservative but feel uncomfortable with Southern Christian evangelism.

As I wrote earlier I am a Deist like many of our Founding Fathers, and I own that perspective here. Many of the Founders were themselves tolerant of, but rejecting the imposition of revealed religious traditions they believed were claiming false superiority.[4] I believe the American Restoration Movement would be wise to adopt a religious pluralist position that upholds Nature's God without requiring belief in doctrinal religious imperatives that can sometimes lead to division. The Founders created a republic that had its basis in Nature's God and was tolerant of many different religions and sects and even those people that were not believers. This necessarily pluralistic attitude certainly did not impose religious exclusivity on its citizens in either law or tradition. It might even be said that Deism has always been the de facto "national" religion of America even though the vast majority of Americans are professed Christians as they were at the time of our founding.

I would like to encourage my Liberal friends in human services and academia or those that identify with the progressive political tradition because they have distaste for what they see as narrow-mindedness, as in the above critique, to reconsider Classical Liberalism. We need you in the Restoration Movement. The Progressives are using you to take the country off a cliff so they can rebuild a different nation. They are using the tools of cultural Marxism to co-opt the energy that you feel because of the cultural divide above to foster a transformative agenda, an agenda I do not believe you really want. I am especially speaking to my African-American, Gay, academic and feminist friends and colleagues who are a part of the pluralistic American community our Founders created. Please consider learning more about the American Restoration Movement, remain true to your core values, but also join us in deconstructing Progressivism and restoring America.

The Obama campaign was an ingenious covert sales job that thankfully yielded buyer's remorse when the middle of the country started to see what it entailed in real terms. Most independent voters had no idea what candidate Obama meant by a "fundamental transformation of America." Now it is clear it is a Marxist/Socialist transformation.

As of today only about thirty-eight percent of likely independent voters supports President Obama's agenda.[5] Now that much of the Conservative base is activated, there is a powerful grass roots movement afoot to stop and reverse the agenda that the Progressive establishment in Washington, lead by President Obama, is attempting to enact. Conservative leaders in Washington and around the country are getting the message. As the above data shows, most independents are no longer expressing support for a blank slate Obama.

It is critical that the American Restoration Movement accelerates now because this is our opportunity and it may never come again. Conservatives still have a majority in the United States but that majority is diminishing because of demographic changes and other factors, so time is running out to restore the country to its founding ideals.

As I wrote earlier, this effort is already well underway and is best represented by the Tea Party Movement, which I believe is the most significant cultural expression in America since the opposition to the Viet Nam war in the 1960's and 70's. In many ways, it is an even more powerful expression than the anti-war movement because it is staunchly *for* a set of core Constitutional values that are timeless and transcendent.[6] There is a renewed excitement for Classical Liberalism and finally, the populist energy to awaken those transcendent values.

Activists in the anti-war movement defined themselves by what they were against, an unpopular war. An amorphous *peace* became the alternative to the Viet Nam War but the peace principle did not offer the Constitutional fortitude that the values behind the American Restoration Movement do today. Tea Party protesters, and others affiliated with the American Restoration Movement, love the United States of America and they stand firmly with the principles that make up her core identity. Everyone believes in peace, but those of us in the Restoration Movement believe peace can never be achieved without a more foundational societal commitment to freedom. In this respect, we believe President Bush was correct. The American Restoration Movement holds that the United States, with its foundational commitment to liberty, is the best hope for creating a peaceful world.

We are at a tipping point in American history. As I wrote earlier, I believe the misguided election of President Obama will be the impetus the quiet majority in America needs to enact a bold, restorative agenda. As history tells us, it usually takes a bold action to create a counter-reaction and in this case, it has taken the election of an ideological Progressive President, who many see as uninspired by our traditional values, to usher in a rabid democratic pro-American-identity protest. People are waking up to the inspiration and the Truth of the American Constitution and speaking truth to entrenched power. I am glad to be a part of that energy and hope this book will contribute to the cause of freedom.

Destroying the Hippie Fantasy (Again)

President Obama seems like a decent man, albeit undoubtedly corrupted by the agnosticism, apathy, anti-Americanism, and moral relativism of our X'er Generation (I am a year older than President Obama), much of that fueled by high rates of drug and alcohol abuse without the social conscience of the prior generation. We had the sex, drugs, and rock and roll without the accompanying social causes. It was an age of narcissism.

The late 1970's brought us disco, leisure suits, and increasingly unimaginative rock music that came at a time of economic despair and lack of faith in much of anything. The President Carter years brought us economic stagnation, a decline in nationalism, and a sense of impotence in world affairs. Apathy reigned in America and in some ways, it defined my generation as we looked around and tried to make sense of the world. My hunch is the cultural malaise of the 1970's may have affected Barack Obama as it did many of us Generation X'ers who were teenagers during that era. His agenda seems to point to a philosophy that is ambivalent or even cynical about the United States.

Many of us grew up with a subtle anti-Americanism and nihilism that our boomer predecessors and Progressive teachers hoisted upon us. Cynicism was high. Many of us tuned out and did not care about anything besides sports or drugs, which were our favorite recreational pursuits. Is it a coincidence that President Obama seems to spend an inordinate amount of his political capital talking about sports? The highest incidence of marijuana use on record was in 1979, which was the year Barack Obama graduated from high school.[7] Pot provided us with an easily available self-destructive protest against conventional norms. This was not a good time to be a youth in America. I have often joked that I believe the United States would be smart to skip over our entire generation when it selects its political leaders. Many of us are damaged goods and it is showing today in the way we are governing.

Obama came of age in that era and in my opinion, it seems that he may be suffering from what I like to call, generational envy. Many of us who grew up in the 1970's wanted to be like our hippie predecessors because we thought they were cool and we admired their radical spirit. However, the late seventies was an era of agnosticism and cynicism in which the country was recovering from the turbulence of the prior era and wanted to avoid conflict. The country was not in the mood for continued activism, and thus we had few outlets for our idealism, which lead to a sense of frustration and envy. We felt cheated and we were bored. That malaise often showed itself in self-destructive behavior.

We looked to our predecessors for approval and we tried to emulate their actions. If only we knew the things that we admired were characteristics of what is now considered by some social commentators as a self-absorbed generation, we could have dismissed our childish notions and found our own identity.[8] However, we thought they were so cool and that envy stayed with many of us into our adult lives.

Many of us moved past this hippie envy and made our own path when we woke up to the truth about the hippies. For many of us this change of heart happened when we formed our own families and became participating members of our communities. For the first time in our lives, we were joining rather than tuning out. However, some of us may still be stuck in that adolescent time warp, especially if we lack exposure to alternative ideas. The empty, utopian rhetoric I hear coming from President Obama indicates to me that he may still be a victim of that hippie envy and looking to half-grown, false prophets around him for Truth. This also suggests to me why President Obama may be having trouble leading with authenticity. His ideas are not his own, nor are they connected to enduring, positive American values. Nevertheless, alas, he is the powerful President of the United States.

The end of the Obama Presidency in 2012 will be the final nail in the coffin for the hippie fantasy and will bring about the acceleration of the American Restoration to undue over one hundred years of Progressivism. That movement peaked in the 1960's was mortally wounded when the Soviet Union fell in 1991, and has been dying a slow death since then until this last burst of utopian dreaming in the failed Obama years. This is not to say there is not to this day a robust Progressive Movement with its Marxist/Socialist and underground Communist sympathizers in the United States. There still is such a presence, and it has been growing during the Obama years, but the ideology can be defeated if Conservatives rise up once and for all and overwhelm it with renewed energy, better ideas, electoral defeats, and sound policies. A lot of damage will have been done by the time the Obama era ends and much work will need to be done to reverse the destruction to our national character, but the mission will be clear and the motivation will be high.

Realistic Optimism on the Rise

The post-progressive years will be lead by realistic optimists who have discarded outdated progressive notions of what constitutes human progress. The ranks of the disaffected Liberals will grow and a new generation of common sense realists will continue to assume the center of American political and social life. Pro-Americanism will be cool again and will attract people from all walks of life, creating a pragmatic governing coalition that will set the stage for the Millennial ascendancy in America.

The realistic optimist activists will be Common Sense Independent Conservatives from the producer class, or disaffected Liberals, many of them young Americans, that have become disillusioned at how far the United States has strayed from its Constitutional roots. They will be the modern day common sense philosophers. The letter below from an anonymous American citizen writer to the *Daily Reckoning*, a Libertarian-leaning investment newsletter, expresses the frustration and common sense approach of these folks well:[9]

"I went down to Chile in 2008 with the idea of just vacationing and learning Spanish. I found to my surprise that Chile is a great country and an economic power in its own way. It has low government debt, etc. Anyway, I found a job with a tech company making about 15 percent less than I was making in the U.S., but my money went so much further. I was able to buy a 2-bedroom 2-bath condo with all the amenities and 24/7 security for about $120,000 U.S. dollars. There was also no income tax. Basically you just pay a 19 percent sales tax on everything. It was just so simple to live there. The government left you alone and expected you to work for what you got. They also have a privatized retirement plan where you pay 12.5 percent of your check to a company who manages your stock portfolio for you. Then you pay 7 percent for your private medical care comparable to U.S. health care. It was nice to never have to fill out any tax forms and to keep roughly 80 percent of my paycheck every pay period."

As this person indicates there are places to live around the world that offer more freedom and simplicity than the United States and still within a capitalistic economic framework. Successful entrepreneurs are growing weary of the increasing complexity and regulation of our current regulatory, high tax, and lawyer-driven system. We need to solicit the ideas and support of people like this writer and other producers while marginalizing the voices of the Entitlement class and the Progressives if we are to restore the productive foundation in America. The United States is a meritocracy that needs to reward risk taking and success rather than stagnation and mediocrity.

The People Rule

There are many independent grass roots groups like A Place for Possibilities emerging daily from the renewed energy in our democratic process. Most are excited about the prospects of a return to limited government with less corruption and with a renewed respect for Constitutional American ideals. Many are ideological but non-sectarian, energized for change based in enduring American Truths, but respectful of differences of opinion about how to get there. This patriotic revival mirrors what was happening in the days immediately preceding the American Revolution. These are exciting times in the United States of America and I am glad to be living in this era.

The American community I talked about in Chapter One is not a nostalgic, *Leave it to Beaver* figment of our imaginations. This is the way life used to be for most Americans even in areas of the country that are now overrun by blight. Families were stronger, neighborhoods were more cohesive, and people acted with more personal responsibility. I believe we can recreate the American community if we take some bold steps now and have the courage to follow through in the face of what will be very intense, perhaps even violent opposition from the keepers of the status quo. There are many people that have an enormous stake in the government-corporate oligarchy, and those folks will not step aside easily. They will need to be defeated by Common Sense Conservatives in an ideological and electoral war, a war that is already raging.

There is a sea of discontent sweeping across the land that longs for the America it used to know and love. That is the energy that is driving this Restoration Movement, a movement that is weary of illegitimate and misguided attempts to perfect our union. The people's movement seeks to revitalize the spirit of the Constitution and Declaration of Independence, a return to liberty, personal responsibility and reverence for Nature's God. Many citizens are learning about our national heritage for the first time and how far we are straying from the core beliefs of the great men that started America. These energized citizens are becoming fearful and angry as they realize we are losing our core identity. Those emotions are driving the desire to stand up and put a stop to the socialist slide.

I believe this may be the first time since before the Great Depression that the majority of Americans is prepared to vote for people that will cut their own entitlements, although a recent poll may still suggest that many Americans are not ready for personal sacrifice.[10] There is a growing recognition that the federal government has overstepped its Constitutional bounds and has become its own special interest group.[11] This development signifies a sense of desperation for some and a spiritual awakening for others who have finally decided to put aside their own self-interests for the good of the country. Others are simply dismayed by the state of the economy and want things to be better. Whatever the reason, these are consequential times in America and a sea of change is on the horizon.

The primary fear of American voters today is the national debt.[12] Even some of our political leaders are starting to get it and act with courage in the face of status quo self-interest. Republican Governor Chris Christie of New Jersey is the best example to date of a leader who seems to understand what must be destroyed and what should be restored in America.[13] I hope Christie will run for national office. Moreover, there are more significant heroes emerging on the local level in smaller governing enclaves. This is ground zero for the Community Restoration Movement in America. When the people lead the government will follow.

In 2011, the quiet majority in America is still strong enough to withstand the progressive onslaught that has been creeping forward for over a century, but time is running out. Progressives have been buying votes and building allegiance with public spending and brainwashing for many decades and that strategy is reaching its pinnacle now under President Obama and this Progressive Congress. Constitutional Common Sense Conservatives must stand up have their voices heard now in public forums, in the media, in social networking sites, and at the voting booth. This is how the restoration will occur — one conversation at a time, wherever the opportunity presents itself to change hearts and minds. We need to speak truth to power and act in the community interest rather than advocate for our limited self-interests. We must be exceedingly careful to avoid conflicts of interest that will diminish our message and compromise our integrity. At times, we will be advocating for things that will negatively affect our own bottom-lines. We need to stand for what is right and true. This effort is for our children and grandchildren.

In my way of thinking about this strategy, it means speaking up for freedom, personal responsibility, voluntary neighborliness, and thrift at every opportunity. When we assess situations as community leaders, we need to advocate courses of action we believe will lead to the advancement of these principles. That means thinking deeply about the ramifications of our actions so we can implement practices we believe will work. It means we will need to stand up to the inevitable peer pressure from status quo interests who resort to guilt tripping and fear mongering to get what they want. We must ignore the inevitable cries of racism and sexism and the claims that our advocacy will hurt children and other vulnerable people. We must see those accusations as political rhetoric intended to further the self-interests of people who are benefiting from the current illegitimate system or who want to transform America into a socialist state. We must offer sound arguments without bombast and monitor our own emotional reactivity. It will take considerable courage and a thick skin to speak truth to power as it always has.

CHAPTER TWELVE

Big Changes in the Economic System

Consistent with my belief that we are at a tipping point in American history in which our liberty is disappearing because of an expansion of government and related corporate interests, my restoration plan is largely a call for a widespread deconstruction of institutions that drink at that well. It is time to subtract rather than add. Others are focusing on reconstruction through addition. It is not that I am opposed to any new growth or reforms and indeed some of the reconstruction ideas have merit, especially in transportation and infrastructure. However, in a society that is economically and morally bankrupt our priority should be getting back to basics by deconstructing what is not working and rebuilding our economic and moral infrastructure, based on an enduring set of values.

Columnist David Brooks talks about the need for clear values in a recent *New York Times* editorial entitled, "Ben Franklin's Nation".[1] Mr. Brooks believes that as the world changes, the United States will need to be able to define itself by its values rather than by its rank, which is a position that mirrors my own thinking. In the post-American world, the American identity will still be important, or even more important as the world becomes increasingly interconnected. We will need to remember who we are and be comfortable sharing our values without the fundamentalist nationalist attitude that has dominated international discourse in the past. In my way of thinking, the Post-American world will be one in which Americans are free, well differentiated, congruent, and neighborly.

In an inspiring new book, Prince Hans Adam II of Liechtenstein writes that it is indeed possible to unwind the mega-welfare state to return the state to its primary functions. Prince Adam believes those essential functions are: providing for the national defense, educating its people through a voucher system, and ensuring the rule of law. In *The State in the Third Millennium*, Prince Adam advocates a systematic deconstruction process, which would involve devolving the power of federal governments and related programs so local communities would be better able to serve their citizens. In contrast to how much of Europe now operates, Prince Adam envisions the state as a *service company* whose limited role is to serve and protect its citizens as efficiently as possible. I find this concept appealing and believe it represents what most Americans want from their government.

Unfortunately, the century long progressive ascendancy in the United States Government and its related proxy institutions has created a dependency state that will be difficult to deconstruct. Today, over twenty percent of Americans is in some way dependent on direct government subsidy for housing, food, or welfare.[2] That percentage will rise precipitously if the recently passed Health Reform Law is enacted. Many more Americans are receiving government subsidy in one form or another if we include corporate welfare, nonprofit organization grants, government worker salaries and military personnel costs. That percentage is difficult to calculate but some observers believe it may be greater than fifty percent of all Americans and rising.[3] This figure is a new high that reverses a self-reliance trend that started under Reagan in 1980.

Consequently, it will take some time to unwind the socialist buildup. Nobody knows what the optimal intensity or duration for an undertaking like this should be because it has never been attempted on such a large scale in the history of the world. There have been many periods of austerity that balanced excesses of previous economic bubbles but there has never been a wholesale societal deconstruction in a Liberal democracy such as what will be needed to restore America during this crisis. In my opinion, Americans are fearful but the majority of us are now ready for such a dramatic undertaking.

Remember, the Marxists believe the current economic condition is an expected and necessary evolution. They have no inclination to change anything. They await the revolution. Change too soon could create a revolutionary fervor and backlash among those that have come to believe that Uncle Sam owes them something – or better stated that it is appropriate for Uncle Sam to take earnings from some people and give it to them. Many stakeholders are brainwashed by those that keep their power by maintaining the status quo. Like any dependency, going cold turkey could be dangerous. So, it will be important for our leaders to make a firm commitment to a fundamental change of direction, as I will explain below, but to make the changes gradually so as to reform the system in a manner that our fragile economy and the dependents in it can handle. That is not to say there will not be any pain. We have made our own bed and now it is time for us to sleep in it. Each of us is going to have to sacrifice something.

The new American center is making its core beliefs well known and they are angry. They distrust big government and they distrust big corporations. They see both entities as corrupt, inefficient, and essentially broken. My belief is we have an unholy alliance between government and large corporations that needs to be put asunder. When push comes to shove and we are forced to make a decision I believe we should always err on the side of freedom from government as our Founders warned. Consequently, while I see both government and corporations as co-conspirators in the modern day oligarchy I believe it is government power, more than corporate excess that we should fear the most.

Formerly the American political system had organized itself around a false polarity. One party was the party of business and the other was the party of government. The new center is exploding that notion and is making it clear they do not trust either party because each ensures its own political power by aligning with the corrupting influences from both of those powerful special interests. The new center, represented by Conservative Populism generally, wants to reign in the excesses of corrupt corporations AND government. I support that balanced perspective and believe it is the key to restoring American liberty, opportunity, prosperity, and happiness.

The best way to immediately affect our broken community would be to starve the government sponsored and union money interests in the human services sector to reduce waste, bureaucracy and professionalization. Public safety net advocates and Libertarians should be able to agree that if public services are deemed to be necessary, the best way to help people is to get the resources and services to them directly and with as little middle man interference as possible. Unfortunately, that is not the case today because we have powerful civil service unions and a self-perpetuating services sector jobs economy getting in the way and blocking efforts to streamline the delivery system. It is often said in jest by serious reformers that we would be better off standing on the street corner and handing out one hundred dollar bills to people rather than subjecting them to the layers of our awkward and inefficient human services system.

Some government reform reports have concluded that if we closed several ineffective federal government departments and streamlined others, returning those functions to states and local communities like our Founders intended, we could save trillions of dollars per year in waste and inefficiency.[4] Most Americans support this action and want the federal government to have less power and less money.[5] Returning control of functions and mandates currently managed by the federal government to local communities encourages ownership, empowerment, neighborliness and personal responsibility. Common sense tells us that most communities would do better without the interference and unfunded mandates.

In my opinion, even impoverished communities would improve if they could get control over their own lives and get the federal government out of their business.

We need to eliminate the lion's share of government sponsored human services programs, returning to the America of the early twentieth century that believed in voluntary neighborliness. In essence, we need to advocate for the dismantling of the early Progressive Era, New Deal, and Great Society programs that have done so much to increase entitlement and destroy American communities. In so doing we will need to ignore the fear mongering that will come from the left. When we look through the lens of personal responsibility we will advocate for conditions that lead to a diminishment of entitlement and reliance on collective over personal responsibility. This is where the rubber meets the road in America. We need to recreate a social welfare system that fosters personal responsibility and voluntary neighborliness instead of social justice and professionalization. This is what our Founders had in mind when they envisioned the United States of America and it is the restorative direction we need to take today.

As importantly, we need to find ways to reduce the corruption, inefficiency, and soul-killing effects of mega corporations in America. We do not support the strong-arming and probably unconstitutional actions of the judicial and legislative branches of government that are popular with many Liberal Populists today and seem more directed at demonizing corporations for political purposes rather than reforming them. There are some factions in America that want to destroy all private corporations in favor of community and worker ownership of all means of production, which is a communist position and one I do not support. Some are conjecturing that President Obama leans toward a communist position, which is a scary thought and one that would be the biggest scandal in the history of the country. I believe citizen action and Constitutional governance can be applied to limit the corruption and inefficiency in corporations that have contributed to an increasingly soul-less and cynical American community. However, I believe corporations are an important part of the American capitalistic system.

I support streamlining labor laws and initiating tort reform against excessive lawsuits. This enactment would free up corporations to hire people to further their missions to make products and deliver services that people want and need rather than managing risk and responding to government regulations. Most companies today are so encumbered with defensive practice and red tape that the lawyers rather than the corporate leaders are running the organizations. This has created a distrustful atmosphere in organizations where entitlement and "getting mine" is the order of the day. The sense of mission that every business needs to be successful has evaporated in favor of short-term gains.

I believe all corporate welfare and government incentives handed out to businesses are unconstitutional and should be abolished. This includes energy and farm subsidies. If a business cannot make it on its own, it does not deserve to exist. The free market should decide which businesses succeed or fail and we should never be afraid to see a business fail because a failure cleans out the market for future business successes. Every failure is painful as is every loss in life, but all losses are also opportunities for change and growth.

In order to jump-start our economy and create private sector jobs so we can get away from government entitlement and serfdom we should reduce payroll, capital gains, and all business income and profit taxes. The corporate taxes in the United States are among the highest in the world, which is creating a non-competitive condition with other countries.[6]

I support a national strategy to revitalize the manufacturing sector of our economy and a corresponding reduction of the services sector, which is bloated and harmful to community wellbeing as I wrote earlier. This is a massive undertaking that will be greatly enhanced if the above actions are taken along with federal investment in infrastructure, more realistic labor compensation laws, better trade policies, and an improved educational system.

These areas of potential government intervention offer addition by subtraction. Further explication of the specifics of this revitalization effort is beyond the scope of this book. I do not believe we can restore America without revitalizing our manufacturing base because in large part America needs to put men back to work. See my ideas earlier about the growing imbalance in the American workforce.

Another area where there is strong public support for spending cuts is in foreign aid. In a recent Harris Interactive Poll, seventy-two percent of Americans believed aid to developing countries should bear the greatest spending cut burden.[7] This was the largest percentage found in the poll. Most Americans believe we should not be borrowing money in order to give it to other countries. I support the notion, advanced by some policy-makers that aid should be given only when it is in the clear strategic interest of the United

States. Even though foreign aid accounts for a relatively small percentage of the overall federal budget, cutting back would be an important symbolic gesture and it would begin to send a different message to the world, that the United States is no longer the world's Sugar Daddy.

When looking through the lens of personal responsibility we should evaluate the extent to which aid given to foreign governments is encouraging long-term independence and economic sustainability instead of perpetuating an international American welfare state. The international situation mirrors the domestic condition in which citizens in prosperous and responsible states like Texas are being told they must bail out the citizens in irresponsible states like California. A country cannot survive if it consistently rewards corruption and irresponsibility by redistributing wealth from its responsible people to the less responsible. Americans are generous people but in this situation, their common sense tells them our priorities are misaligned. It is time to reign in international welfare.

I believe small business is the backbone of the United States. Small businesses create jobs, community ownership, and neighborliness. Small businesses will benefit from the reforms suggested above and will greatly benefit from a freer, and more entrepreneurial spirit in the nation. As importantly, the American people can support their communities by buying local (even if they need to pay a little more) from small businesses that are more apt to employ their neighbors and to have a stake in the local communities.

I support the burgeoning *Buy Local Movement*, which encourage citizens to buy goods and services in their own neighborhoods whenever possible, even if they have to pay a little bit more, and encourages businesses to buy local in return. We have an active coalition in Portsmouth, New Hampshire that is coordinated by a nonprofit organization called *Seacoast Local.*[8] In addition to the benefits of encouraging neighborliness and supporting small businesses, Environmentalists also believe the buy local approach improves environmental sustainability. I like this idea because it is voluntary and local. It strengthens local businesses and fosters a decentralized and less mega-corporate economy, which is consistent with the ideals of our Founders and the goals of Conservative Populism.

I support most of the austerity measures that fiscal Conservatives are advocating and especially a flat sales tax system commonly known as the *Fair Tax* that would give everyone a direct stake in America rather than cynically dividing Americans into producer and parasite classes. Today, according to the nonpartisan Tax Policy Center, forty seven percent of Americans paid no federal income taxes in 2009.[9] That does not include the estimated between ten and twenty million illegal immigrants and others in the underground economy who are working for cash under the table and paying no income taxes, or the income underreporting from some small business enterprises that results in lower collection rates.[10]

The class warfare arguments from the proponents of income tax progressivity serve the needs of Marxists who maintain power by keeping people angry and victimized. A simpler, flatter, tax system would go a long way toward simplifying the lives of Americans and restoring some confidence in our country. Every study I have seen shows that a

flat sales tax would actually increase federal tax revenues because it would cut down on underpayments due to income
underreporting, under the table employment schemes,
fraud, and tax sheltering.[11] A flat tax would further reduce
professionalization and bureaucracy as well because it would
put a lot of tax preparers and IRS agents out of business and
it would help people feel more directly connected to the
goods and services their taxes are funding. Like all of the
reforms I am suggesting, there would be short-term pain
but long-term benefits to society. The well-researched and
detailed fair tax proposal is on the table now (see related
footnote) and could be implemented quickly.

Most importantly, I support serious cuts of at least thirty
percent in social welfare entitlement programs, the largest of which is Medicaid, which is in reality a jobs program
for government-sponsored workers who tend to vote for
Progressive candidates. Medicaid is bankrupting state budgets all over the country and if we would seriously measure
the outcomes of Medicaid funded programs I believe we
would find they are similar to Head Start, an abysmally ineffective program that is funded year after year despite a
series of independent outcome studies that demonstrate its
lack of efficacy.[12]

There is probably no bigger detriment to the health of
the United States than the exploding welfare state. Fraud
and abuse alone in these programs accounts for billions in
expense to taxpayers.[13] As in Europe, we are reaching a tipping point where the majority of Americans could be on
some form of government welfare assistance or government
sponsored employment for their daily sustenance.[14] In real

terms that means the producers of revenue are shrinking and the receivers are growing, which is an unsustainable pattern. In addition, it means that America is shifting from a nation of merit to a nation of entitlement, which is transforming America to a social welfare state.

As unpopular as it will be to recipients and constituent special interest groups, I support a substantial reduction in all social and corporate welfare programs in order to correct this imbalance. This would also improve the relationship between producer/taxpayers and legitimate welfare recipients. Right now, primarily due to the perception of rampant fraud and abuse in these programs and the belief that too much of the money is going to bureaucrats and providers rather than recipients, there is very little trust between many taxpayers and service recipients.

The best way to reform systems is to reduce their funding because it has the effect of shrinking their excesses and forcing a more efficient application of resources. More importantly, it would open up more opportunities for voluntary neighborliness, which as I have said, should be a national priority.

I also support a Baby-Boomer give back in Social Security where Baby-Boomer seniors (those reaching the retirement age this year) would see their benefit cut by as much as thirty percent. Since Baby-Boomers have benefited from the largess of the American economy more than any group in history and have sacrificed the least in my opinion, it makes sense for them to take less now so the system can be maintained for the more elderly seniors and saved for their children and grandchildren. Older seniors would see their benefits remain the same. Baby-boomers will need to work longer by necessity to make up for the shortfall and families will be forced to stay in communal living longer in order to create economies of scale. This change will contribute to a more neighborly society where all people will be forced to help each other out more in order to survive.

I support reductions in the government-sector pension programs at the federal, state, and municipal levels, which were in large part unfunded liability promises made to public workers essentially in exchange for votes. Municipalities, states, and the federal government offered fantasy money they never had that was based on a fantasy credit, bubble-economy. All the while our banks and our governments were borrowing, laundering, and printing money to make it look like we were all rich so we could spread the money around for everyone with no limit. We have reached the end of the line to the tune of one hundred thirty trillion dollars in unfunded liabilities nationwide.[15] Government pensions are a big part of that unfounded liability and unfortunately, there is no choice but to cut them now.

Many of these pensions built up over time as the economy rolled along in the bubble years. states, municipalities, and the federal government provided benefits that were too rich in an ill-conceived effort to keep up with the bubble-generated private sector gains during the 1990's and 2000's. However, as private interests lost money, the state, local, and federal governments did not react accordingly to cut generous allotments because they are beholden to service employee unions and various other political interests that control most government jobs. Now, when the United

States is on the verge of bankruptcy, governments must ad-
just those pensions downward to keep up with deflationary
pressures. That means telling recipients the system is broken
and the money is not there — as George Bailey did in that
famous scene at Bailey Savings & Loan from the classic mov-
ie, *It's a Wonderful Life*. All of us must accept personal sacrifice now if the economy is to survive.

I support reductions in military spending in weapons systems curtailments, personnel cost reductions, and base clo-
sures around the world and especially in Europe. The United
States can no longer afford to be the global policeman and
the NATO protector because we have nearly bankrupted our
economy doing it. It is time that European and other prosperous nations contribute a larger share of the defense burden around the world. Modern warfare methods are more
efficient and less costly if we take the necessary steps.

There may be an emerging consensus among many in
the political classes that this needs to be done, especially
since the libertarian and traditional Conservative voices
are getting more prominent throughout the political landscape, thus aligning with Liberals who have always wanted
to reduce the size of the military budget. The next Congress
needs to act courageously in this matter and not allow special interests to dissuade prudent action.

In healthcare reform, I believe we should replace the
current employer or government-sponsored single-payer
and managed care systems with a new individual-based system that would promote personal responsibility. Medicaid
and Medicare must be included in these reforms. I advocate a return to the idea that health insurance is "insurance"
against a catastrophic condition.

The average American could purchase a private policy of their choosing from anywhere in the country that offered one hundred percent coverage for medically necessary hospitalization and a co-insurance offset for serious, costly, outpatient procedures. Consumers with means would pay for all routine outpatient procedures out of pocket. In order to achieve this goal, states and the federal government would need to relax existing regulatory intrusion that limits options and choice. The federal government would employ strict income means testing to determine eligibility for the Medicare and Medicaid benefits. Those programs would also close the loopholes that currently allow children from families with means to be eligible for Medicaid. Finally, the federal government would combine the administrative management of the two programs to save bureaucracy costs.

In this new system, the impetus for cost control and quality assurance would rest with the consumer where it belongs. It would also reduce costs in the healthcare system dramatically, which is the primary goal of healthcare reform. This change would lead to people visiting their doctors only when necessary and would encourage them to engage in healthier habits because they would realize they were paying dearly for their irresponsibility. The new system would benefit providers and consumers, greatly simplifying the process by removing many of the overseers and bureaucrats from both the public and private systems who add little value and a lot of complexity and cost. My plan returns personal responsibility and thrift to healthcare, lowers costs, improves health, and covers more Americans.

The restoration of America cannot occur without serious cuts to big-ticket economic items that make up the bulk of the thirteen trillion dollar national debt and one hundred thirty trillion in unfunded liabilities. Making these cuts would be painful initially but the actions would forestall a complete meltdown of the capitalistic system. Some economic Libertarians and other austerity proponents like Congressman Ron Paul agree that if our leaders do not take these actions soon they will happen automatically in the near future as a result of bankruptcy.[16] Rather than waiting for bankruptcy to occur, a prudent approach would dictate an intentional and well-planned process that will minimize damage.

Leaders in government will need to decide on the timing of the preferred austerity program in order to maximize benefits and minimize negative consequences. This will be painful but we need to look at the long term, and leaders must be willing to risk their professional futures. It is promising that due to the recent Congressional election it appears there will be a lot of new citizen legislators, many influenced by the Tea Party Movement, that are entering citizen government to do their jobs and go home when they are done as our Founders had intended. It will take that level of personal integrity and courage to get the job done. More importantly, as I have tried to illustrate above, in the long-term, these serious systemic interventions would both support and encourage the restoration of freedom, personal responsibility, neighborliness, and thrift on the road to a better America.

AFTERWORD

Individuals Being the Change
They Want to See in the World

While I believe the restoration of America is not possible without a dramatic deconstruction of institutions, fueled by a serious outcomes evaluation of all programs and across the board spending cuts, I do not believe making such changes is itself the key to restoring a better America. America will be restored when the preponderance of individuals begins to live with honor and integrity. We have become a society that functions on denial, greed, hypocrisy, conspicuous consumption, cynicism, and destructive entitlement. Many of us live in a near constant state of psychological denial, in which we compartmentalize our immoral decisions in order to justify them. When more people begin to live an honorable life the culture will change and institutional health will follow.

The deconstruction and rebuilding of institutions and services that make up the government-corporate oligarchy and a return to personal integrity will stimulate a revival of the civil society, which is the bedrock of America. When the civil society begins to reign again, it will be because we have rediscovered freedom, personal responsibility, neighborliness, and thrift. In addition, it will serve as a bulwark against the tyranny of the authoritarian impulse as it always has. The civil society will again supplant the Progressive onslaught that seeks control of our citizens and our communities in order to empower central governments and enrich those that benefit from that enterprise. These will be happy days in America like that which we have not seen since the aftermath of World War II.

The tragic, realistic, inevitability is that many people will not be able to make the transformation to a life of integrity and honor. Many people have never lived such a life. In the short run, there will be an increase in acting out and lawlessness as people begin to realize the gig is up and the gravy train is over. This is scary. Nevertheless, it is going to happen. We need to prepare our families and our communities.

The restoration of America is a spiritual journey that begins and ends with individual people doing the right thing most of the time because they want to be good people. While it is convenient for us to blame our politicians or corporations or certain segments of society for the deterioration of our country, in actuality the enemy is in the mirror. We are the politicians, the corporations and "those people" and we made our own bed. Sure, there are powerful forces and political movements that have amassed or exploited their power for illegitimate or nefarious ends. However, all change begins with us and we have the power to change the American culture by sowing those seeds of personal change everywhere. As Mohatma Gandhi said, we need to be the change we want to see in the world.

We begin the deconstruction, re-moralization, and restoration of America today. We Baby Boomers and Generation X'ers really made a mess of things and now we have a moral responsibility to clean it up before we turn the reigns over to the Millennials.

If we do the hard work now, this next greatest generation will rediscover the beauty of America and give her to the world in the way our Founders intended. They have the right combination of courage, compassion, optimism, practicality, and realism to accomplish what the previous Greatest Generation did during World War II, to save humanity from its own narcissistic and controlling instincts. There is no guarantee the Millennials will be successful, but I have the faith of a proud father that they can be – if those of us in positions of influence today, do our part now so these Millennials have a chance to do great things in the future.

APPENDIX

A Place for Possibilities
Responsive Community Resources Inc.
117 Bow Street, Suite 111, Portsmouth, NH 03801
www.aplaceforpossibilities.org
aplaceforpossibilities@gmail.com

A 501 (c) 3 educational nonprofit corporation dedicated to building a better community by fostering the American ideals of freedom, personal responsibility, neighborliness, and thrift.

If you would like to support our nonprofit mission below, kindly send a tax-deductible contribution of any amount to: RCRINC, 117 Bow Street, Suite 111, Portsmouth, New Hampshire, 03801. All of the proceeds from *Discovering Possibility* are being used to advance the mission of A Place for Possibilities.

Philosophy

Common Sense Conservatism also known as Yankee Libertarianism, or Classical Liberalism

We believe The United States of America is a Country of boundless opportunity. Our Declaration of Independence states that all men are created equal, that they are endowed by their Creator with certain unalienable rights, that among these are life, liberty and the pursuit of happiness. That to secure these rights, governments are instituted among men, deriving their just powers from the consent of the governed.

Thus, we believe free men and women have a right to pursue their dreams as they choose and that FREE INDIVIDUALS, exercising their LIBERTY and acting in concert with one another and with limited professional interference have the best chance at creating healthy and prosperous communities. We believe UNCHECKED CENTRAL GOVERNMENTS eventually give in to the controlling and narcissistic impulses of man so we believe America should be in a constant state of DECENTRALIZATION, DECONSTRUCTION, and RESTORATION. We believe a LIMITED CENTRAL GOVERNMENT has a right to manage institutions erected for the common good, in order to provide for the common defense and to protect the RIGHTS GUARANTEED in the U.S. Constitution, and ONLY THOSE RIGHTS guaranteed by the Constitution. We believe individuals are happier and communities prosper when individuals embrace both their rights AND THEIR RESPONSIBILITIES as good citizens and good neighbors and thus we believe in the concept of ORDERED LIBERTY which demands that in a free society there must also be a vibrant civil society that through its families, communities of faith, and cultural institutions, promotes VOLUNTARY personal responsibility, neighborliness, and thrift.

What makes us unique?

With so many emerging grass roots organizations out there what makes A Place for Possibilities different? Many libertarian leaning organizations are too close to anarchy for our comfort. Many exist for the advancement of key causes that do not interest us like legalization of drugs, gun rights, or freedom from taxes. While these are valid issues, they do not represent the passion behind our beliefs, which are more communitarian and emphasize personal responsibility and the social responsibilities we believe we have toward each other in order to allow freedom to reign without too much central planning.

We are a non-sectarian, non-religious organization and while we embrace the notion of natural rights as guaranteed by our United States Constitution, we do not require supporters to subscribe to a religious test, nor do we exclude anyone that does not believe in God. We advocate the advancement of what we believe are universal Truths inscribed in our Declaration of Independence and United States Constitution because we believe they are bedrock principles that lead to individual happiness and build healthy communities.

Our niche

There are many excellent organizations already bringing their messages to settings that are sympathetic to restorative American ideals. Our transparent goal is to change the hearts and minds of people that are Progressive leaning because of tradition, peer-pressure, or politics. We believe the philosophy outlined above, that can also be called a classical liberal position, has been stigmatized by political Progressives and media as "uncool" and thus is too easily dismissed by folks that otherwise might be attracted to Common Sense Conservatism. The word, "conservative" scares some people. In addition, we believe our Deistic emphasis appeals to folks who have common sense conservative convictions, including belief in a higher power, but do not wish to be identified as part of a particular religious community.

We try to accomplish our goal through education and assertive thoughtful persuasion, which is a method deeply rooted in our democratic American tradition. The Internet is the modern day printing press, and thus we embrace the full power of this new media to advance our message. Consequently, we believe in using thoughtful persuasion in the best American democratic tradition to attempt to influence our neighbors to adopt the community-enhancing ideas we love.

We do not believe it is in the community interest to pressure our legislators to pass more laws to make everyone behave in more community friendly ways. There are enough laws on the books already. Instead, we need to change the culture, one conversation at a time. As the culture changes our political process will follow and the laws will begin to reflect the restorative beliefs of the American people.

We are nonsectarian *Free Spirits for Truth and Common Sense* that offer an alternative voice within the professional communities that tends to favor entrenched politically Progressive ideologies, which are at odds with the time honored American ideals above. We are deeply concerned that professional helpers, academics, and social entrepreneurs, by accommodating to the dominant Progressive ideology, are contributing to an increasingly authoritarian, irresponsible, entitled, and socialistic society.

We employ state of the art Internet resources and traditional face-to-face methods to reach professional helpers who otherwise might not be exposed to this message because of the one-sided politically correct ideology that dominates our professional discourse.

ACKNOWLEDGMENTS

I would like to acknowledge my wife, Karen, for her moral support on this project, especially in the face of some anticipated criticism from those that might disagree with the book's premise, and for her stellar copyediting. In addition, since we grew up in the same town and have now shared a lifetime of experiences, Karen and I wrote Chapter One together. My son Brian also helped with formatting and research. My daughter Lauren inspires me daily with her adventurous, independent spirit and passion for living.

My parents, Dan and Claire Kervick, cultivated in me the unusual combination of a free spirit with a simultaneous respect for tradition and values, a personality make-up that is at the core of my identity and is the basis of the Common Sense Conservatism in this book. My siblings, Dan, Chris, and Anne Marie, each gave me the support and challenge that allowed me to believe I could attempt such a task as writing a book filled with my own ideas.

My in-laws, Ernst and Inge Frevel, both immigrants from Germany in the 1950's, inspire me by their very presence, as their personal histories are remarkable.

There have been many thoughtful colleagues, mentors, media influences, and friends throughout my career both in the face-to-face and Internet worlds who encouraged me, stimulated my thinking and helped to shape my ideas. I did not always agree with them, nor did they always agree with me but I benefited tremendously from the creative energy that comes from spirited discussion. A few of them are my former business partner, Donna Tonrey, and a community-building collaborator, David Weiskotten. Scott Miller and William Doherty have been inspirational mentors for me because they went beyond their clinical identities as mental health professionals to attempt to change the culture.

While I do not know Glenn Beck, I have found his courage to seek and spread controversial ideas in the face of tremendous opposition to be inspiring. Beck's knowledge of history and powerful issue advocacy added fuel to my fire, thus pushing me to finalize this book. While I may not be completely aligned with Mr. Beck spiritually, in my opinion, he is one of America's greatest culture change agents, a community builder extraordinaire.

I have relied heavily on three organizations, *the Institute for American Values*, *the Communitarian Network*, *and the Coalition for Marriage, Family, and Couples Education* (Smartmarriages), for social science research and information for over a decade. Each of these organizations has been on the cutting edge of what I would call the Common Sense Conservative Movement in America, although many of the thought leaders in those organizations would probably not identify themselves that way.

Finally, I would like to thank the Creator for offering a world so full of beauty and awe that I was inspired to try to contribute to the effort to make it a little bit better.

BIBLIOGRAPHY

The following books were among the most influential in shaping my thinking for Discovering Possibility.

Beck, Glenn. *Common Sense: The Case Against an Out-of-Control Government*. New York: Pocket Books, 2009.

Blankenhorn, David, Barbara Dafoe-Whitehead, Sorcha Brophy-Warren. *Franklin's Thrift: The Lost History of An American Virtue*. West Conshohocken, PA: Templeton Press, 2009.

Etzioni, Amitai. *The New Golden Rule*. New York: Basic Books, 1996.

Hans-Adam II Prince. *The State in the Third Millennium*. London: I. B. Tauris, 2009.

Hoff-Sommers, Christina. *Who Stole Feminism? How Women Have Betrayed Women*. New York: Touchstone / Simon & Schuster, 1995.

Howe, Neal and William Strauss. *Millennials Rising, The Next Great Generation*. New York: Vintage Books, 2000.

Keen, Sam. *Fire in the Belly: On Being a Man*. New York: Bantam, 1991.

Levin, Mark. *Liberty and Tyranny: A Conservative Manifesto*. New York: Threshold Editions, 2009.

McKnight, John. *The Careless Society: Community and its Counterfeits*. New York: Basic Books, 1996.

Meacham, Jon. *American Gospel, God, the Founding Fathers, and the Making of a Nation*. New York: Random House, 2006.

Newberry, Tommy. *The War on Success, How the Obama Agenda is Shattering the American Dream*. Regnery Publishing: New York, 2010.

Paine, Thomas. *The Age of Reason*. Edited by Philip S. Foner. Secaucus, NJ: Citadel, 1974.

Putnam, Robert. *Bowling Alone: The Collapse and Revival of American Community*. New York: Simon Schuster, 2000.

Romney, Mitt. *No Apology: The Case for American Greatness*. New York: St. Martin's Press, 2010.

Seligman, Martin. *Authentic Happiness*. New York: Free Press, 2002.

Thoreau, Henry David. *Walden; or Life in the Woods*. Boston: Ticknor and Fields, 1854.

Wiker, Benjamin. *10 Books Every Conservative Must Read: Plus Four Not to Miss and One Imposter*. Washington DC: Regnery, 2010.

AUTHOR BIOGRAPHY

Kevin Kervick is a social entrepreneur, author, presenter, possibilities coach, mentor, and organizational development consultant with an extensive background in marriage and family therapy and human services leadership.

For the past twelve years, Kevin has been working primarily as a community-capacity builder and trainer for A Place for Possibilities, which is an educational nonprofit corporation he founded in 2005, and as a consultant/trainer for other groups, including an international organization that supports the United States Military.

His recent polemic, *Interpersonal Wisdom, the Capacities and Characteristics of the Best Talk Therapists*, published in the forward-thinking *New Therapist Magazine*, a South-African publication, was well-received as a visionary, iconoclastic view and call to action.

Kevin publishes three blogs. *Kevin's Korner* is a common sense wisdom blog for coaching clients and anyone interested in adopting ideas that lead to personal happiness and wellbeing. *Free Spirits for Truth and Common Sense* is a social action blog for Common Sense Conservative community builders and the communication arm for A Place for Possibilities. *Kevin Kervick's InterpersonalWisdom*, is a blog for talk therapists and coaches that reviews the transtheoretical best practices capacities and characteristics of excellent talk therapy guides and other helping professionals.

Kevin has been married to his high school sweetheart, Karen (Frevel) for twenty-seven years and they have two grown children, Lauren twenty-five, and Brian, twenty-four. Kevin and Karen currently reside in Portsmouth, New Hampshire.

NOTES

Introduction: Restoring America - A Place for Possibilities

1   Jeff Landauer and Joseph Rowlands, *Importance of Philosophy Website*, last updated 2001; available at: http://www.importanceofphilosophy.com/Bloody_PositiveRights.html. Since the concept of rights limits the actions of the government, the only way to circumvent them is by adding new rights that are allegedly superior to the others. The concept of Positive Rights was developed. These new rights differ from the old rights. Instead of involving freedom from interference from others, these new rights demand goods and services. "Positive" refers to the fact that to satisfy these rights, other people must provide them.

2   Kate Zernike, *Boiling Mad: Inside Tea Party America* (New York: Times Books, 2010).
Information about the origins of the Tea Party Movement was included in a presentation Ms. Zernike gave at River Run Bookstore in Portsmouth, New Hampshire on October 12, 2010.

3   Kate Zernike, "Rep. Ron Paul, GOP Loner, Comes Out from the Cold," *New York Times*, December 12, 2010; available at: http://www.nytimes.com/2010/12/13/us/politics/13paul.html?pagewanted=2&_r=1&nl=todaysheadlines&emc=a2.

4   *The Rally to Restore Sanity and Fear* was a well-publicized and well-attended rally organized by Jon Stewart and Stephen Colbert of the *Comedy Central Network* in Washington D.C. on October 30, 2010; Morley Winograd and Michael D. Hais, *Millennial Makeover: My Space, YouTube and the Future of American Politics* (New Brunswick: Rutgers University Press, 2008), 92-93.

5   A Fasnacht is a fatty doughnut treat served traditionally on Fasnacht Day (Shrove Tuesday), the day before Lent starts.

Chapter 2 - Freedom Around the World

1   Keanu Sai, David Keanu Sai v. Barack Obama, et. al., 2010; available at: http://hawaiiankingdom.org/sai-obama.shtml.

Chapter Three - The Civil Society

1   Much of the information in this section is corroborated by: Thomas West and William Schambra, "The Progressive Movement and the Transformation of American Politic," The Heritage Foundation, *First Principles Project*,

2007; available at: http://www.heritage.org/Research/ Thought/fp12.cfm.

2 Herbert Marcuse, *An Essay on Liberation* (Boston: Beacon Press, 1999). The victim narrative is an expression of cultural Marxism that attempts to place the feminist, civil rights, and peace movements as within the class struggle dialectic of Classical economic Marxism (emphasis mine).

3 I am using a term that was coined by: Scott MacFarlane, *The Hippie Narrative: A Literary Perspective on the Counterculture* (Jefferson, North Carolina: McFarland & Co. Publishers Inc., 2007), 1-8.

4 Karin Asbley, et. al., "You Don't Need a Weatherman to Know Which Way the Wind Blows," *New Left Notes* (June 18, 1969).

5 Taken in part from: Ernest Barker, ed., *Social Contract* (London: Oxford U. Press, 1960). Contains essays: John Locke, *An Essay Concerning the True Original, Extent, and End of Civil Government*; David Hume, *Of the Original Contract*; and Jean-Jacques Rousseau, *The Social Contract*.

6 Taken from the letters of Thomas Jefferson to Abigail Adams (February 2, 1787) William Smith (November 13, 1787) and related works of Jefferson.

7 "48% See Government Today as a Threat to Individual Rights," Rasmussen Reports, June 24, 2010; available at:

http://www.rasmussenreports.com/public_content/politics/general_politics/june_2010/48_see_government_today_as_a_threat_to_individual_rights.

8   "Only 21% Say U.S. Government Has Consent of the Governed," Rasmussen Reports, February 18, 2010; available at: http://www.rasmussenreports.com/public_content/politics/general_politics/february_2010/only_21_say_u_s_government_has_consent_of_the_governed.

9   Friedrich Hayek, *The Road to Serfdom* (London: Routledge Press, 1944), Chapters 10-13. The definition of Classical Liberalism I am using in this context can be found in Hayek's seminal work although there are many other excellent sources.

Chapter Four - Deism Revisited

1   Deism is knowledge of God based on the application of our reason on the designs/laws found throughout Nature. The designs presuppose a Designer. Deism is therefore a natural religion and is not a "revealed" religion.

2   David Holmes, *The Faiths of our Founding Fathers* (New York: Oxford, 2006), 28-50. Russell Shorto, "How Christian Were the Founders?" *New York Times Magazine* (February 11, 2010): 6; available at: http://www.nytimes.com/2010/02/14/magazine/14texbooks-t.html.

3   John Adams, Speech to the U.S. Military (1798).

4   Robert L. Johnson, *The Deist Roots of the United States of America*, accessed December 13, 2010; available at: http://www.deism.com/deistamerica.htm; Lewis Loflin, *A Critical Examination of Deism*, accessed December 13, 2010; available at: http://www.sullivan-county.com/deism.htm.

5   Thomas Jefferson, *The Existence of Deity*, *The Jeffersonian Cyclopedia*, John P. Foley, ed., (New York: Funk and Wagnalls Company, 1900).

6   Thomas Jefferson, *The Life and Morals of Jesus of Nazareth* (Washington, D.C.: United States National Museum, 1895).

7   Ira Stoll, *Samuel Adams: A Life* (New York: Free Press, 2008), 4-6, 9-11.

8   Benjamin Franklin, Letter to an unknown recipient (December 13, 1757) (Sometimes mistakenly attributed as a letter from Franklin to Thomas Paine).

9   Michael McCullogh and Brian Willoughby, "Religion, Self-regulation, and Self-Control: Associations, Explanations, and Implications," *Psychological Bulletin* 135, no. 1 (2009).

10   Paul Taylor, Cary Funk, and Peyton Craighill, "Are We Happy Yet?" Pew Research Center: *A Social Trends* Report, February 2006; available at: http://pewresearch.org/pubs/301/are-we-happy-yet.

Chapter Five - Societal Devolution

1   Steffen Ganghof, "The Politics of Tax Structure," Max Planck Institute, 2006; available at: http://www.mpi-fg-koeln.mpg.de/people/ga/Dok/Yale_revised.pdf.

2   This claim comes from direct conversations I had with several people in 2009 from the former East Berlin, Germany.

3   C. S. Lewis, *God in the Dock: Essays on Theology and Ethics*, ed., Walter Hooper (Grand Rapids, MI: Eerdmans Publishing, 1970), 292

4   Bill Bonner, "Spitting on the Boomers' Financial Legacy," *The Daily Reckoning Newsletter*, November 2009; available at: http://dailyreckoning.com/spitting-on-the-boomers-financial-legacy/.

5   W. Bradford Wilcox, Elizabeth Marquardt, "The State of Our Unions Annual Report,"The National Marriage Project of the University of Virginia (2010) available at: http://www.virginia.edu/marriageproject/.

6   David T. Ellwood and Christopher Jencks, The Spread of Single Parent Families Since 1960, John F. Kennedy School of Government, Harvard University, 2002; available at: http://www.sociologycentral.com/sptext/family/read/singleparentspread.pdf.

7   National Fatherhood Initiative research data on the consequences of father absence, accessed December 13, 2010; available at: http://www.fatherhood.org/Page.aspx?pid=403.

8   Sara McLanahan, "Family Structure and the Reproduction of Poverty," *American Journal of Sociology*, 90, no. 4 (1985): 873 (Chicago: The University of Chicago Press).

9   Maggie Gallagher, "The Age of Unwed Mothers, Is Teen Pregnancy the Problem?" The Institute for American Values, 1999; available at: http://www.americanvalues.org/Teen.PDF.

10   *The Marriage Movement, A Statement of Principles*, The Institute for American Values (2000) available at: http://www.americanvalues.org/pdfs/marriagemovement.pdf.

11   Stephanie Coontz, *The Way We Really Are: Coming to Terms with America's Changing Families* (New York: Basic Books 1997), 2

12   Rich Morin, and D'Vera Cohn, *Women Call the Shots at Home, Public Mixed on Gender Roles*, Pew Research Center, September 5, 2008; available at: http://pewresearch.org/pubs/967/gender-power.

13   William Bennett, "Quantifying America's Decline," *Wall Street Journal*, March 15, 1993; available at: http://www.columbia.edu/cu/augustine/arch/usadecline.html.

14   William Doherty, Putting Family First (New York: Henry Holt, 2002), 3

15   Kimberly Young, "Treatment Outcomes with Internet Addicts," *CyberPsychology & Behavior*, 10, no. 5 (2007).

16   "*Media Bias 101*: What Journalists Really Think - and What the Public Thinks About the Media," Media Research Center, October, 2009; available at: http://www.mrc.org/static/uploads/MediaBias101.pdf.

17   Thomas Edsall, "Journalism Should Own its Liberalism, and then Manage It, Challenge It, or Account for It," *Columbia Journalism Review*, October 8, 2009; available at: http://www.cjr.org/campaign_desk/journalism_should_own_its_libe.php; "Many Say Coverage is Biased in Favor of Obama," *Pew Research Center*, June 5, 2008; available at: http://people-press.org/report/427/many-say-coverage-is-biased-in-favor-of-obama.

18   Jonathon Strong, "Documents Show Media Plotting to Kill Stories About Rev. Jeremiah Wright," *The Daily Caller*, July 20, 2010; available at: http://dailycaller.com/2010/07/20/documents-show-media-plotting-to-kill-stories-about-rev-jeremiah-wright/print/.

19   A. Leslie Morrow, ed., "Alcoholism and Obesity: Overlapping Brain Pathways?" Bowles Center for Alcohol Studies, *Center Line Newsletter*, 14, no.1 (March 2003)

available at: http://www.med.unc.edu/alcohol/center-linenews/documents/Vol14_No1.pdf.

20   The Free Dictionary; available at: http://www.thefreedictionary.com/statism. Statism is the theory or practice of concentrating economic and political power in the state, resulting in a weak position for the individual or community with respect to the government.

21   David Batty, "Debt Crisis: EU Leaders Announce €70bn Plan to Protect Euro," *The Guardian* (May 8, 2010).

22   Ronald Reagan, *A Time for Choosing*, Televised speech (Los Angeles, CA) airdate October 27, 1964; transcript available at: http://www.americanrhetoric.com/speeches/ronaldreaganatimeforchoosing.htm.

Chapter Seven – Freedom

1   "Only 17% Say Today's Children Will be Better Off Than Their Parents," Rasmussen Reports, December 9, 2010; available at: http://www.rasmussenreports.com/public_content/business/general_business/december_2010/only_17_say_today_s_children_will_be_better_off_than_their_parents.

2   Adrian Worsfold, *Freudian Psychology in Brief*, accessed December 13, 2010; available at: http://www.change.freeuk.com/learning/socthink/sfreud.html. Libidinous energy is a component of Drive Theory, which concludes that

humans are motivated by aggressive and sexual "drives" (ID) to seek power and restrained by social conscience (Superego).

3   Ibid.

4   Wikiquote Contributors, United States, "Edmund Burke," *Wikiquote*, accessed December 13, 2010; available at: http://en.wikiquote.org/wiki/Edmund_Burke.

5   Kevin Kervick, *Kevin's Korner* (blog) Available at: http://kevinkervick.wordpress.com.

6   Hannah Fenichel Pitkin, "Are Freedom and Liberty Twins?" *PoliticalTheory*, 16, no. 4 (November, 1988) 523-552.

7   Ronald Inglehart, Robert Foa, Christopher Peterson, and Christian Welzel, "Development, Freedom, and Happiness: A Global Perspective," *Perspectives on Psychological Science*, 3, no. 4 (1998): 264-285.

8   K. Christensen and B. Schneider, eds., *Workplace Flexibility: Realigning 20th Century Jobs to 21st Century Workers* (Ithaca, NY: Cornell University Press, 2010): 274-308.

9   The Free Dictionary, accessed 12/14/10; available at: http://www.thefreedictionary.com/introjects. Introjection means to incorporate characteristics of a person or object into one's own psyche unconsciously.

10   Lyman Wynne et. al., "Pseudomutuality in the Family Relations of Schizophrenics," *Psychiatry*, 21 (1958): 205- 220. Pseudomutuality refers to a dysfunctional family condition that is characterized by false intimacy.

11   Thomas Paine, *The American Crisis*, no. 4 (1777).

Chapter Eight - Personal Responsibility

1   Tommy Newberry, *The War on Success* (Regnery Publishing: New York, 2010), 36.

2   David Horowitz and Jacob Laksin, *One-Party Classroom: How Radical Professors at America's Top Colleges Indoctrinate Students and Undermine Our Democracy* (New York: Crown Forum, 2009), 1-6

3   Christina Hoff-Sommers, *Who Stole Feminism? How Women Have Betrayed Women* (New York: Touchstone / Simon & Schuster, 1995), 22. "Gender feminism is a gynicentric and misandric branch of feminism." Gender feminists typically criticize contemporary gender roles and aim to eliminate them. In current usage, "gender feminism" may also describe feminism, which seeks to use legal means to give preference to women in such areas as domestic violence, sexual harassment, divorce proceedings, and pay equity (emphasis mine).

4   Hanna Rosin, "The End of Men," *The Atlantic Magazine*, July/August 2010; available at: http://www.theatlantic.

com/magazine/archive/2010/07/the-end-of-men/
8135/.

5   Classical feminism fought against genuine violations
of women's rights while modern (gender) feminism has
turned into a male-bashing elitist club.

6   Tom Huppi, *A Review of Keynesian Theory*, accessed
12/13/2010; available at: http://www.huppi.com/kanga-
roo/Keynesianism.htm.

Keynesian economic theory advocates active public sector contributions in order to stabilize economic downturns
created by insufficient private sector activity.

7   Ben Quinn, "UK Budget 2010: New Era of Austerity
in Europe?" *Christian Science Monitor* (June 22, 2010).

Chapter Nine – Neighborliness

1   Murray Bowen, *Family Therapy in Clinical Practice*
(New York: Jason Aronson, 1978). I am using neighborliness
in the same way that Murray Bowen, noted family therapist,
talked about the capacity for relationship because of a well-
developed differentiation of self.

2   Marion F. Solomon, *Narcissism and Intimacy: Love and
Marriage in an Age of Confusion*

(New York: W. W. Norton, 1989), 135. A fundamental tenet of object-relations theory, an outgrowth of psychoanalysis, is that relationship distress is connected to early life developmental problems that have one growing up fearing abandonment or engulfment.

3   Durkheim's depiction of anomie is available at: http://en.wikipedia.org/wiki/Anomie.

4   Robert D. Putnam, "E Pluribus Unum: Diversity and Community in the Twenty-First Century," The 2006 Johan Skytte Prize Lecture, *Scandinavian Political Studies*, 30, no. 2 (2007): 137–174.

5   Wikipedia Contributors, United States, "United States Public Debt" *Wikipedia, The Free Encyclopedia*, accessed December 13, 2010; available at: http://en.wikipedia.org/wiki/United_States.

6   John McKnight, *The Careless Society: Community and Its Counterfeits* (New York: Basic Books, 1996), 8.

7   Ivan Illich, *Medical Nemesis: The Expropriation of Health* (New York: Pantheon Books, 1976), 39, 211, 262.

8   Mark Tyrrell, "Major Depression Facts," *Clinical-Depression.co.uk*, accessed December 13, 2010; available at: http://www.clinical-depression.co.uk/dlp/depression-information/major-depression-facts.

Benjamin Scafidi, "The Taxpayer Costs of Divorce and Unwed Childbearing," Combined report from the Institute for American Values, Georgia Family Council, Institute for Marriage and Public Policy, and Families Northwest (2008).

9 *Discovering Possibility* Transformation System for Human Services Organizations, available at: https://home. comcast.net/~kervick/discoveringpossibilityprogram.htm.

10 Kevin Kervick, *Free Spirits for Truth and Common Sense*, accessed December 13, 2010; available at: http:// freespiritsfortruthandcommonsense.blogspot.com.

11 Maria Shriver et al., "The Shriver Report: A Woman's Nation Changes Everything," Report from the Center for American Progress, 2009; available at: http:// www.americanprogress.org/issues/2009/10/pdf/awn/a_ womans_nation.pdf.

Chapter Ten - Thrift

1 Wikipedia Contributors, "Economy of the United States," *Wikipedia, The Free Encyclopedia*, accessed December 13, 2010; available at: http://en.wikipedia.org/wiki/ Economy_of_the_United_States.

2 Origin of the term unknown.

3 Jay Hefflin, "Majority of Americans Oppose the Bailout of Greece," *On the Money, The Hill Finance and Economy*

Blog, May 17, 2010; available at: http://thehill.com/blogs/on-the-money/801-economy/98153-majority-of-americans-oppose-the-us-bail-out-greece.

4 "Monthly Treasury Statement." Department of Treasury Financial Management Services, May, 2010; available at: http://www.fms.treas.gov/mts/mts0510.pdf.

5 "Influence of Consumer Dept on Bankruptcy Filings," American Bankruptcy Institute, August, 2007; available at: http://www.abiworld.org/statcharts/CDebt.pdf.

6 "U.S. Courts Bankruptcy Statistics," United States Courts, April 2010; available at: http://www.uscourts.gov/FederalCourts/Bankruptcy.aspx; "National Economic Accounts" Bureau of Economic Analysis; available at: http://www.bea.gov/national/.

7 Steve Conover, "International Debt Thermometer," *The Skeptical Optimist*, accessed December 13, 2010; available at: http://www.optimist123.com/optimist/2007/06/international_d.html.

8 Tim Kasser, Allen D. Kanner, eds., *Psychology and Consumer Culture: The Struggle for a Good Life in a Materialistic World* (Washington, D.C.: American Psychological Association, 2003), 13, 29.

9 Clifford E. Thies, "The Paradox of Thrift RIP," *The Cato Journal*, 16, no. 1 (Spring/Summer, 1996) available at: http://www.cato.org/pubs/journal/cj16n1-7.html.

10   The Institute for American Values is an independent organization whose mission is to strengthen fundamental American values. Available at: http://www.americanvalues.org/; David Blankenhorn, "There is No Paradox of Thrift," *Weekly Standard*, 14, no. 37 (June, 2009) available at: http://www.weeklystandard.com/Content/Public/Articles/000/000/016/592bjsid.asp.

11   Eda Gurel-Atay, et. al., "Changes in Social Values in the United States: 1976-2007; Self-Respect is On the Upswing as A Sense of Belonging Becomes Less Important," *Journal of Advertising Research*, 50, no. 1 (2010) 57-67.

Part Three Introduction - The Hard Work of Restoring the American Community

1   New World Encyclopedia Contributors, *New World Encyclopedia*, accessed December 13, 2010; available at: http://www.newworldencyclopedia.org/entry/Axial_Age.
Axial Age is a term coined by German philosopher Karl Jaspers to describe the era from 800 BCE to 200 BCE. The pace of change today and what some consider to be a confluence of interconnected social, economic, and spiritual factors, taken together with increasing globalization and communications, leads some to believe this is a new Axial (pivotal) era (emphasis mine).

2   Nedra Klein Weinreich, "What is Social Marketing?" *Weinreich Communications*, 2006; available at: http://www.social-marketing.com/Whatis.html. Social marketing is a

communication method that seeks to influence social be-
haviors not to benefit the marketer, but to benefit the target
audience and the general society.

Chapter Eleven - Free Spirits for Truth and Common Sense

1 Bill Bonner, "The Long and Short of The Great
Correction," *The Daily Reckoning Newsletter*, April 01,
2010; available at: http://dailyreckoning.com/the-long-
and-short-of-the-great-correction/.

2 Fareed Zakaria, *The Post-American World* (New York:
W. W. Norton, 2009). *Post-American* refers to a world in
which many other countries are catching up to the United
States in terms of economic power. In the case of President
Obama, the term has been used by some to question his be-
lief in American Exceptionalism (emphasis mine).

3 "In 2010 Conservatives Still Outnumber Moderates,
Liberals," *Gallup Organization*, June 25, 2010; available at:
http://www.gallup.com/poll/141032/2010-conserva-
tives-outnumber-moderates-liberals.aspx.

4 Thomas Jefferson, *The Life and Morals of Jesus of Nazareth*
(Washington, D.C.: United States National Museum,
1895); Thomas Paine, *Of The Religion of Deism Compared
With the Christian Religion*, *Life and Writings of Thomas Paine*,
Daniel Edwin Wheeler, ed., (New York: Vincent Parke &
Co., 1908).

5   Jeffrey M. Jones, "Obama Job Approval Rating Down to 38% Among Independents," *Gallup Organization*, July 7, 2010; available at: http://www.gallup.com/poll/141131/obama-job-approval-rating-down-among-independents.aspx.

6   Scott Graves, *The Contract from America*, December 13, 2010; available at: http://www.thecontract.org/2010/09/the-contract-from-america/.

7   Jennifer Lloyd, "Drug Policy Information Clearinghouse Fact Sheet," Report from the Office of National Drug Control Policy, October, 2002; available at: http://www.whitehousedrugpolicy.gov/publications/factsht/druguse/.

8   Paul Begala, "The Worst Generation," *Esquire Magazine* (April 1, 2000); Steve Gillon, *Boomer Nation: The Largest and Richest Generation Ever and How it Changed America* (New York: Free Press, 2004), 20.

9   Eric Fry and Joel Bowman, eds., "Getting Outta Dodge," *The Daily Reckoning Newsletter*, June 21, 2010; available at: http://dailyreckoning.com/getting-outta-dodge/.

10   "Americans Want Government to Spend for Jobs, Send Bill to Rich," Bloomberg Polling, December 3-7, 2010; available at: http://www.bloomberg.com/apps/news?pid=newsarchive&sid=awkrRPMONDW8.

11   "Only 21% Say U.S. Government Has Consent of the Governed," Rasmussen Reports, February 18, 2010; available at: http://www.rasmussenreports.com/public_content/politics/general_politics/february_2010/only_21_say_u_s_government_has_consent_of_the_governed.

12   Lydia Saad, "Federal Debt, Terrorism Considered Top Threats to U.S.," *Gallup Organization*, June 4, 2010; available at: http://www.gallup.com/poll/139385/Federal-Debt-Terrorism-Considered-Top-Threats.aspx.

13   Chris Christie, *Conversation with the Governor* (Ramsey, NJ) March 24, 2010; available at: http://www.youtube.com/watch?v=nceBCFEiivQ; *Doing More with Less* (Bayonne, NJ) March 17, 2010; available at: http://www.youtube.com/watch?v=_BeINHucpgc&NR=1.

Chapter Twelve - Big Changes in the Economic System

1   David Brooks, "Ben Franklin's Nation," *New York Times*, December 14, 2010; available at: http://www.nytimes.com/2010/12/14/opinion/14brooks.html?_r=1&nl=todaysheadlines&emc=a212.

2   William Beach, "The 2009 Index of Dependence on Government," Report from The Heritage Foundation, March 4, 2010; available at: http://www.heritage.org/

research/reports/2010/03/the-2009-index-of-dependence-on-government.

3   Mark Trumbull, "As U.S. Tax Rates Drop, Government's Reach Grows," *The Christian Science Monitor* (April, 2007).

4   Fred Thompson, "Government at the Brink, Volume 1: Urgent Federal Management Problems Facing the Bush Administration," Committee on Governmental Affairs, U.S. Senate (Washington, D.C.: June 2001) available at: http://hsgac.senate.gov/vol1.pdf.

5   "62% Say Politicians Want Government to Have More Power and Money," Rasmussen Reports, June 21, 2010; available at: http://www.rasmussenreports.com/public_content/politics/general_politics/june_2010/62_say_politicians_want_government_to_have_more_power_and_money.

6   Dan Mitchell, "Politicians Fiddle While America's Corporate Tax System Burns," *International Liberty Website*, October 30, 2009; available at: http://danieljmitchell.wordpress.com/2009/10/30/politicians-fiddle-while-americas-corporate-tax-system-burns/.

7   "Spending Cuts are Preferred to Higher Taxes to Reduce Deficits in the U.S., Great Britain, France, Italy, Spain, and Germany," Financial Times/Harris Interactive

Polls, July 14, 2010; available at: http://www.harrisin-
teractive.com/NewsRoom/HarrisPolls/FinancialTimes/
tabid/449/ctl/ReadCustom%20Default/mid/1512/
ArticleId/438/Default.aspx.

8   Karen Marzloff and Tom Holbrook, *Seacoast Local
Website*, accessed December 13, 2010; available at: http://
www.seacoastlocal.org/.

9   Roberton Williams, "Who Pays No Income
Tax?" *Tax Facts From the Tax Policy Center*, June 29,
2009; available at: http://www.taxpolicycenter.org/
UploadedPDF/1001289_who_pays.pdf.

10   Steven Camarota and Karen Jensenius, "A Shifting
Tide: Recent Trends in the Illegal Immigration Population,"
Report from the Center for Immigration Studies, July, 2009;
available at:http://cis.org/IllegalImmigration-ShiftingTide.

11   Leo E. Linbeck, Jr. and Robert C. McNair, *The
Fair Tax Website*, accessed December 13, 2010; available at:
http://fairtax.org.

12   *Head Start Impact Study*, Final Report to the Office
of Planning, Research, and Evaluation, Administration for
Children and Families of the U.S. Department of Health and
Human Services, January, 2010; available at: http://www.
acf.hhs.gov/programs/opre/hs/impact_study/reports/
impact_study/executive_summary_final.pdf.

13   "Medicare Fraud, Waste, and Abuse: Challenges and Strategies for Preventing Improper Payments," U.S. Government Accountability Office (Washington D.C.: Government Printing Office, June 2010); "Medicaid: Fraud and Abuse Related to Controlled Substances Identified in Selected States," U.S. Government Accountability Office (Washington, D.C.: Government Printing Office, September 2009).

14   Exact figures are not known. But since 2008, as the national deficit and debt figures indicate (See below), the federal government has increased its ownership of formerly private enterprises and its social welfare payments and associated bureaucracy (emphasis mine).

15   *U.S. National Debt Clock Website*, accessed December 13, 2010; available at: http://www.usdebtclock.org/.

16   *Ludwig von Mises Institute Website* available at: http://mises.org/.

INDEX

www.ingramcontent.com/pod-product-compliance
Lightning Source LLC
Chambersburg PA
CBHW062144280526
45788CB00001B/293